T0272986

Ordination

Moksananda

Ordination

WINDHORSE PUBLICATIONS

Published by Windhorse Publications
11 Park Road, Birmingham, B13 8AB

© Moksananda 2004
Printed by Interprint Ltd
Marsa, Malta
Cover design: Marlene Eltschig
Photograph of Punyaruci's ordination by Vidyalila
Detail of rose: © Royalty-free / Corbis

British Library Cataloguing in Publication Data:
A catalogue record for this book is available from the British Library
ISBN 1 899579 60 5

The publishers wish to acknowledge with gratitude permission to quote poems and extracts from the following:

p.5: Ryokan, *One Robe, One Bowl*, trans. John Stevens, Weatherhill, New York and Tokyo, 1984

p.12: Lucien Stryk (trans.), *On Love and Barley: Haiku of Basho*, Penguin Classics, London 1985. © Lucien Stryk, 1985. Reproduced by permission of Penguin Books Ltd.

p.96: 'Ante el Mar' ('Facing the Sea') by Alberto Quintero Álvarez, from J.M. Cohen (trans.), *The Penguin Book of Spanish Verse*, Penguin Books, London 1988. Copyright © J.M. Cohen, 1956, 1960, 1988. English translation reproduced by permission of Penguin Books Ltd.

Every effort has been made to trace copyright in the following. If any omission has been made please let us know in order that this may be acknowledged in the next edition.

pp.51–2: 'Tiger' by A.D. Hope.

p.96: 'Ante el Mar' by Alberto Quintero Álvarez (Spanish original)

CONTENTS

Más allá de nosotros,
en las fronteras del ser y el estar,
una vida más vida nos reclama.[1]

Beyond ourselves,
on the frontiers of being and becoming,
a more living life claims us.

Octavio Paz

About the Author

Moksananda was born in 1960 in Bournemouth, on the south coast of England. He studied at the University of Warwick, where he gained an honours degree in Economic History, despite being more interested in literature, existential pondering, and playing the bass guitar.

He became a member of the Western Buddhist Order in 1985, and in 1987 moved to Alicante in order to help set up Guhyaloka, a men's retreat centre, in a mountain valley. The following year he travelled to India, where he witnessed the work of the Order among the Dalits (ex-untouchables) and met Dhardo Rimpoche, a leading Tibetan teacher. Both experiences had a profound effect on him, and later that year he moved to Valencia in order to initiate Buddhist activities there. In 1990 he founded el Centro Budista de Valencia (the Valencia Buddhist Centre).

He pays regular visits to Latin America to teach Buddhism, and now works with Spanish- and Portuguese-speaking men to help them train and prepare for ordination. He is private preceptor to a number of such men, and has led a four-month ordination retreat at Guhyaloka during which men from various parts of the world become members of the Order. He now lives in Valencia with his partner and their daughter.

PREFACE

For much of my adult life I have experienced a strong fear of flying – to the extent that I once cancelled a long-haul flight at a day's notice, with no chance of reimbursement, because of my distress at the prospect. The time just before take-off was usually the worst, sitting waiting, with no turning back, strapped in, claustrophobic, berating myself for the stupidity of putting my life at risk again. But remarkably, on this occasion, it was different. I was relaxed, at ease, taking an interest in the final procedures before take-off and in my fellow travellers. Suddenly aware of this difference, I understood the reason for it. A few days beforehand I had been ordained within the Western Buddhist Order. I was not invulnerable, the flight was not certain to arrive, but in becoming ordained I felt I had done the best thing possible with my life, and death – should it come – could not invalidate that.

Fourteen years later, one morning in late summer, I conducted the ordination ceremonies of two women whom I had known for many years. I waited for each of them to arrive for her ceremony in a small wooden hut under the spreading branches of two great beech trees, in the garden of the retreat centre in South Wales where I live and work. Beside me was a beautiful, simple shrine consisting of a small Buddha image, flowers, and candles. Beside it lay a small, blue, spiral-bound book containing the words of the ceremony that we would recite in call and repeat, first in Pali, then in English – in a tradition of ordination going back to time of the Buddha.

I was particularly aware of this sense of lineage as I conducted the ceremonies; aware of my own ordination by a Dhammacāriṇī (Dharma-farer) now in her eighties, and of her ordination by Sangharakshita, the founder of our order, and of his ordination in India some fifty-four years previously. I became aware how the same spark was ignited in the heart of each of us, even though we were of different generations and led such different lives. It was such a spark that impelled the Buddha-to-be to leave the comfort, wealth, and companionship of his home in order to try to penetrate the apparent incomprehensibility of birth and death. Why old age? Why suffering? Why death? Why life? These questions burned in his mind and there was only an intimation of the answer in the sight of a homeless wanderer, a spiritual aspirant, resolved on a quest for the truth, whose bearing in the face of such questions was both purposeful and calm.

The two women I ordained in that simple yet profound ceremony have not literally left home – they both have families and other commitments – but they have gone forth from home to the homeless life by stepping out of a limited view of themselves, and onto a path of transformation unique to each individual but containing a body of teachings and spiritual practices that are universally relevant.

There are now over 1,000 members of the Western Buddhist Order, and many thousands of other Buddhists in various orders around the world. What is it that drew them, and drew me, to ask for ordination and undergo training in preparation? What drew us to commit ourselves to a lifetime of practice directed towards the realization of our full potential as human beings, and the creation of the conditions for others to do the same? Why join an order? What is the significance of a spiritual community? Why not simply meditate and undertake spiritual practices autonomously?

Moksananda, who has been a member of the Western Buddhist Order for eighteen years, has written this book in response to questions from his friends, those who are simply curious, and those who – having felt the benefits of Buddhist practice – want to understand what lies behind that decision, taken by so many diverse people. He explores ordination as a living myth that is as vitally relevant to the lives of twenty-first-century men and women as it was to the followers of the Buddha. He explores ordination as an expression of the universal myth of the quest – the quest for life's meaning – and as a rite of passage initiated not by society but by a shift of consciousness of each individual. In the course of this exploration he relates his own story, his own response to that quest, that call, that glimpse of the 'deathless', and of its beauty; his own experience of ordination, and the journey on which that profound yet mysterious commitment has taken him.

Maitreyi
Tiratanaloka Retreat Centre
Wales
September 2003

INTRODUCTION

Not much to offer you –
*   just a lotus flower floating*
In a small jar of water.[2]

The last few years have seen me living out of a suitcase and clocking up air miles. The suitcase has actually been several, as one after another has succumbed to the rigours of airport handling. Arrival lounges in Spain, Portugal, Britain, Mexico, Venezuela, and Brazil have seen me heaving my case from the conveyor belt, looking for new rips and dents, and heading for the exit (and the waiting customs officers) with a practised air of indifference.

Spending no more than a month in any one place, I have travelled between Europe and Latin America helping others to understand and practise Buddhism. Some of my friends tease me about being a *misionario*, others a wandering monk or sort of spiritual rock star on tour. I can't say I've ever really felt like any of these. Many people seem to find it difficult to understand what I'm doing and why; at times I find it difficult myself. It is not something that is always easy to make sense of in the light of everyday contemporary values.

My friends around the world know that I am a member of the Western Buddhist Order.[3] Many of those I meet for the first time assume I am a monk, though they wonder why I don't wear a habit or sport a shaved head. Young people will sometimes ask me if I'm allowed to have sex or if I have to be celibate. Older people tend to ask me if I'm allowed to get married and have children. Others ask if I am paid to do this work, and if I have to travel to wherever 'they' send me. Occasionally I am asked, by those who assume he is a God, if I pray to the Buddha. I am often either rejected or accepted on the basis of a rather vague belief that Buddhism is a religion, and that somehow all religions are the same.

Indeed, behind many of the questions there seems to lie a basic distrust of religion, in any form, and therefore of what it must mean to be ordained. The truth is that the modern world has inherited an unfortunate history of intolerance and coercion in the name of religion, and is still at times witness to the insidious manipulation of people's lives in the name of religious ideals. Nowadays, many men and women will associate organized religion with dogmatism and fanaticism, or feelings of guilt and fear of punishment. Confusion reigns over what is and what is not historical fact, and inspired myth and symbolism have been literalized into absurd beliefs. Ordained members of different religions have, at times, been seen to take their place within an authoritarian and hypocritical hierarchy and to exploit the power foolishly handed them by 'believers'. In the light of the enormous freedom of choice that many individuals in many parts of the world have nowadays, something of a shadow is cast by religion and those who represent it. It is the shadow of oppression and the abuse of position, of the 'brainwashing' sect and slavery to naive ideologies, of losing the choice to lead one's life as one wishes. There are many who sympathize with the poet-mystic William Blake when he sings:

I went to the Garden of Love,
And saw what I never had seen:
A Chapel was built in the midst,
Where I used to play on the green.

And the gates of this Chapel were shut,
And 'Thou shalt not' writ over the door;
So I turn'd to the Garden of Love
That so many sweet flowers bore;

And I saw it was filled with graves,
And tomb-stones where flowers should be;
And Priests in black gowns were walking their rounds,
And binding with briars my joys and desires.[4]

Though Buddhism cannot be said to be completely free of this spoiling of the Garden of Love, it has nonetheless gained a growing respect and understanding in many parts of the world, and many feel a strong attraction towards what they see as an alternative spiritual tradition.

As I travel from place to place, I again and again meet men and women, young and old, who find in Buddhism a tradition that enables them to give expression to their deepest questions and longings, and a path that gradually leads them to greater happiness. They are often people who simply want to live a meaningful life based on values and principles more enduring than those generally found today. They find that Buddhism offers an approach to life that helps them to do this. Inevitably, many people want to know what it means to be a Buddhist, and some want to understand the significance of being a member of the Western Buddhist Order. So they ask me.

Men and women who join the Western Buddhist Order take part in an ordination ceremony that expresses the essence of what it means to be a Buddhist and a member of this order. This short book has developed from a desire to answer my friends' questions, and in the hope that others will also find it of interest. To explore the ordination ceremony of the Western Buddhist Order is to explore the essence of what it means to be part of this Order, and therefore of one strand of the Buddhist tradition's struggle to take relevant form in the world today. It also means exploring a remarkable rite of passage that reveals universal aspects of spiritual unfoldment.

One of the most vital of human qualities is our ability to sense value: to be able to discern the worth, merit, or importance of a thing. Being a Buddhist is about valuing some things over others, even about having faith in certain things. The value someone assigns to a specific thing or act depends on many factors; each of us has our own hierarchy of values which relate to our ideals and principles, our aims, our cultural conditioning, even our personal taste. What was of importance to us yesterday we might view as having little worth or merit today – and what we disregard today we may come to value above all else tomorrow.

What is valued by those who follow the Buddhist path can be said to be threefold: truth, virtue, and the spiritual potential inherent in all beings.[5] These are of course human values, not specifically Buddhist ones. Buddhism simply emphasizes our innate ability to respond to these values and encourages us to base our lives on them. It encourages us to listen to the sense of conviction that arises when we hear a true word amidst the deafening torrent of untruths and half-truths that sometimes pours down on us. It encourages us to rejoice in the uplifting effect of a straightforward virtuous act amidst the ugliness that often surrounds us. It encourages us to act on the heartfelt longing to live a life through which we might realize deeper dreams and as yet only dimly imagined possibilities.

A Buddhist is someone in whom this sense of conviction, uplift, and longing is sparked off by the Buddha, by his teaching, and by those who follow his example and advice; sparked off to such an extent that he or she actually decides to practise the way taught by him. People who call themselves Buddhists do so because it is in the Buddhist tradition that they personally find truth-teachings, qualities to emulate, and an affirmation of their sense of hidden potential.

Nonetheless, ask any group of Buddhists why they are Buddhists and you will get many different answers. The practice of Buddhism is a deeply personal matter, and each will have their own reasons. We might say that each and every human being is unique, and one's attraction towards the Buddhist tradition reflects that uniqueness.

Within the Western Buddhist Order, as within the Buddhist tradition as a whole, are some who have been primarily drawn to the Buddhist path by a search for truth, a desire to fathom the true nature of life. There are others who have been drawn mainly by the qualities of kindness, love, and compassion which they see reflected in the Buddhist tradition, by the compassionate wisdom that they intuit in the great Buddhist teachers, by the ethical sensitivity that perfumes the Buddhist path, or by the spiritual power that emanates from the figure of the Buddha, deep in meditation. All have probably been drawn to practise Buddhism because the vision of human potential that it upholds resonates with an intuition of their own potential and because they see in Buddhism a way to realize the fullness of that promise.

Some will see themselves as treading a gradual path towards the goal of realizing that spiritual potential, others as attempting to shake off the sleep of ignorance in order to wake to a natural state of clear awareness, others as unfolding the timeless nature of their true selves. Some will be seeking primarily to transform themselves, others to transform the world.

Sometimes Buddhism is described as a philosophy, sometimes as a religion, a psychology, a way of life, or a mystical tradition. It has all these aspects, but is not limited to them. It is clearly rational, and Buddhist philosophy pushes to the very limits of the possibilities of thought; yet it appeals to the heart, and Buddhist devotional and poetic imagery is among the most beautiful in the world. It attempts to fathom the depths of the human mind through a long-standing tradition of psychology, and at the same time it sees that psychology in ethical terms and links the mental states we experience to the way we act. It invites us to explore the many dimensions of consciousness through meditation, yet ultimately it calls on straightforward intuitive awareness so that we may dwell more fully on the mystery of our everyday existence.

In exploring the ordination ceremony of the Western Buddhist Order, and therefore what it means to be a Buddhist and a member of this order, I inevitably reflect my own particular motives, tendencies, and sources of attraction to the Buddhist tradition, as well as my own way of seeing it. I make no apologies for this and hope that, in attempting to explore the meaning of this ceremony on the basis of my own experience, others' sense of conviction, uplift, and unspoken longing may be sparked off.

No doubt my friends, young and old, will continue to have questions. That is also to be hoped for. My answers will not be real answers if they do not throw up deeper and more searching inquiry.

1

RITES OF PASSAGE

In my new robe
this morning –
someone else.[6]

Some years ago I made a special journey. Skirting Mont
Blanc, I walked with a group of friends from France
through the Swiss Alps before making my way south
into Italy and to a former monastery on a low hill beside
a small Tuscan village. The monastery was established
centuries earlier by black-robed Augustinian friars. The
Franciscans later occupied it, until it was partially
destroyed during the Napoleonic wars. Many years later
it was privately purchased and used as a backdrop for
operas, and for a number of years it has been used peri-
odically by the Western Buddhist Order. During the
spring, summer, or autumn months it is the venue for a
special retreat during which people from all over the

world commit themselves to the Buddhist path and join the Order.

The journey I made that summer found its culmination one evening several weeks after I had arrived. Leaving my companions silently meditating together in the meditation hall, I made my way through the building, up stone stairs, and along candle-lit corridors in the half-light of the encroaching night. Everything around me was still, the echo of my footfalls and the flickering candlelight reflecting from the high whitewashed walls and broken terracotta floor; first one corridor, then another, then another, all bathed in candlelight and shadow – until I came to a doorway. I knew that when I entered the room beyond I would, in a sense, never really leave. I also knew that it was in order to enter that room that I had made my journey. I gently pushed open the door and peered in before crossing the threshold.

To one side of the room stood a colourful Buddhist shrine, decorated with flowers, candles, and incense, and a small golden statue representing the Buddha. On a mat to the side of the shrine sat a smiling grey-haired man wrapped in a yellow robe of the Buddhist tradition within which he himself had been ordained. I raised my joined hands in salutation to the shrine, then to the seated man, before he beckoned me to sit on a small cushion in front of him.

As I did so, I knew I was about to do what millions of others had done during the last 2,500 years, since the time of the Buddha. I was about to commit myself to the quest for spiritual awakening and to the path the Buddha had discovered and communicated.

The spirit of the Buddhist tradition, including its teachings and principles, has been kept alive by generation after generation in order to guide others to its goal. The teaching of the Buddha and his followers was preserved and handed down orally at first, then later through the written word. Most importantly, individual men and women have undertaken to tread the Buddhist path. They have lived it out for themselves in a million different ways and have been able to pass on a real understanding of what it means to do so. In front of me sat the man who had become my teacher. Sangharakshita, the founder of the Western Buddhist Order and at that time sixty years old, was about to witness in me, a young man, a commitment that he himself had lived out during the previous forty years.

> To the Buddha for Refuge I go.
> To the Dharma for Refuge I go.
> To the Sangha for Refuge I go.

In the quiet of that candle-lit room, surrounded by the ceaseless chirping of cicadas, I repeated this simple formula.[7] I committed myself to the Buddha, the Dharma, and the Sangha.

Buddhism holds that there are three treasures to which all men and women are heir. The first is the experience of being aware, and the possibility of developing greater awareness, culminating in full intuitive appreciation of the true nature of existence and an unbreakable sense of connection with all beings. This ideal state of loving awareness is known in Buddhism as Enlightenment, and is represented by the Buddha. The word 'Buddha' signifies one who has awoken.

The second thing that Buddhism holds most precious to human life is simply truth, and all that leads to the understanding and embodiment of truth in its many facets. Along with truth, we may say, go beauty and goodness. The ultimate truth is the truth concerning the nature of all things. To realize this truth is to appreciate the essential beauty of all that exists, and to live in accordance with it is to embody the good. In Buddhism this truth is known as the Dharma. It is the truth concerning the nature of existence, and it is also whatever leads to an appreciation of it in its many aspects. It is expressed in all those teachings that make up the Buddhist path.

The third treasure to be found in a human life is the possibility of communication, especially the communication of truth, beauty, and goodness. Communication is an extraordinary phenomenon, allowing as it does for the possibility of sharing consciousness. For the Buddhist tradition, this shared consciousness finds its fullest realization when intuitive awareness of the true nature of life is shared. This experience forms the basis for what is known in Buddhism as sangha, particularly the *ārya* sangha or noble sangha. 'Sangha' can be translated as 'spiritual community'; at its most complete it is noble because it is based on the finest of all shared experience – the experience of reality.

These three treasures, or most precious things – the Buddha, the Dharma, and the Sangha – stand at the centre of Buddhism and are known as the Three Jewels.

Repeating the words of my teacher, words that had come down the centuries, words that filled that very room where we sat, just as the burning sticks of incense filled it with their perfume, I formally committed myself to the Buddhist path. This commitment was both a statement of faith – faith that it was possible to attain Enlightenment or spiritual awakening – and a statement of intention. By the time the short ceremony was over I had reorientated myself towards what I had come to see to be the meaning of life, choosing the path I believed would best enable me to live out that meaning, and undertaking to give expression to that meaning in my communication with others. I had made my own decision concerning what was most important in my life, and my teacher had witnessed my dedication to it. I had given expression to that universal aspiration to understand the nature of life and death and pledged myself to follow the Buddhist path through a simple ritual that would nonetheless affect the rest of my life. The young man that returned to his meditating friends through the half-light of the silent corridors was not the one who had left.

ORDINATION IN THE BUDDHIST TRADITION

This commitment, or pledging of oneself to the Three Jewels, has always been central to the Buddhist path. When the Buddha began teaching some 2,500 years ago there was no organized 'Buddhism'. There were just him, his teaching, and his five ascetic friends. In time his disciples came to include men and women, rich and poor, from all classes of Indian society. Some of them left their families and lived in the forest, practising ethics and meditation, wearing the meagre robes of the wanderers of their time, and begging for their food. Others became followers of the Buddha and practitioners of his teaching while remaining at home with their families. All these disciples of the Buddha were part of the one spiritual community and became part of that community by expressing their allegiance to the Buddha and his teaching.

To begin with, this commitment seems to have had no ritualistic form but to have been something spontaneous that occurred when the Buddha met people and taught them. They would express their experience of suddenly seeing the true meaning of life, or even of experiencing spiritual awakening, by 'going for refuge' to (or 'taking' refuge in) the Buddha – that is, by explicitly devoting themselves to the Buddha, his teaching, and his community of disciples.[8] In time this spontaneous pledge was formulated in a ritual in which the individual expressed this same allegiance to the Buddha, the Dharma, and the Sangha, but now within the context of a more or less developed ceremony.[9]

The Buddhist tradition is today made up of many distinct, though linked, communities and schools, each of which has its own ordination or equivalent, such as monastic ordination for monks and nuns, ordination of novices, forms of lay ordination, and ordination that is common to both monastic and lay followers. Many Buddhist schools have a hierarchy of ordinations. There is a great diversity of approaches, not only to the spiritual path itself but to the expression of an individual's dedication to it. How that diversity has come about is a complex issue open to different explanations and interpretations. What follows is one very simplified account.

This diversity seems to have started early on with the development of different communities. These communities eventually formed different schools which in turn gave rise to the various forms of early Buddhism.

In time there emerged from within early Buddhism two broad movements of thought and practice: the Hīnayāna, or 'lesser way', and the Mahāyāna, or 'great way' (these terms coined, of course, by the Mahāyānists themselves). While recognizing the approach of those they designated Hīnayānists as valid, even essential, the Mahāyānists nonetheless considered it limited. Among other things, they saw that the serious practice of the Dharma was becoming almost exclusively identified with monastic ordination, and the formulation of 'going for refuge' itself, through which the lay devotee still expressed his or her commitment to the Three Jewels, had begun to lose its import. Those who formed the Mahāyāna movement therefore sought ways to express anew the essential commitment to the spiritual quest and to the Buddhist path that constitutes being a Buddhist. This is not to say that the Mahāyāna denied the value or importance of the monastic life, but that the arising of the Mahāyāna reflected, in part at least, a concern that dedication to the Buddhist path had become over-identified with the monastic life to the exclusion of other lifestyles, such as the lay life and that of the forest dweller or wanderer. These Mahāyānists also thought that the practice of the Buddha's teachings had fallen prey to a covert self-centredness and crippling literalism. In a nutshell, the Mahāyāna was a movement which emerged as a response to a perceived narrowing of approach to the spiritual life within early Buddhism. To counteract this, the Mahāyānists developed a more penetrating and poetic philosophy concerning the true nature of existence, emphasized the altruistic and imaginative dimensions of the Buddhist path and of the quest for Enlightenment, and sought to express the core decision of a Buddhist in terms which brought these aspects alive again and freed it from being over-identified with a monastic way of life.

To do this they expressed allegiance to the Buddhist path not only in terms of going for refuge to the Three Jewels, but also in terms of the Bodhisattva vow. This is a vow not only to gain Enlightenment for oneself but also to lead all beings to that same state of spiritual awakening, no matter how inconceivably long that may take and no matter whether one is a monk, nun, lay follower, or homeless wanderer – indeed, irrespective of one's chosen lifestyle. At the same time as establishing this vow to free all beings from spiritual ignorance, the Mahāyānists taught that one should not take literally this idea of self and other. In this way the universal significance of the spiritual quest was revitalized by the Mahāyāna, along with the essential commitment that marks it, and the overall framework of the ungraspable nature of our existence was re-established.

Of course, as time passed, there were developments within the Mahāyāna itself, and a continued natural unfoldment of particular aspects of the Buddhist path. Another broad movement arose: the Vajrayāna or 'diamond way'. If the Mahāyānists had chosen to emphasize the altruistic and imaginative aspects of the Buddha's teaching, the Vajrayānists emphasized both its immediacy and its mystery – even its magic. The Vajrayāna emerged because some practitioners of the Dharma saw the need to re-emphasize Enlightenment as a possibility right now, in this very life. The primary commitment to Enlightenment and the path of the Buddha was therefore given further expression with the introduction of an explicit commitment to the teacher (who was seen as the living embodiment of Buddhahood), on the basis of which the disciple was empowered to undertake particular practices. In many of these practices the follower of the Vajrayāna becomes, at least symbolically and imaginatively, an Enlightened being. Through such practices Enlightenment is emphasized as something that is possible in each and every moment. Spiritual wakefulness is emphasized as innate to all beings and an inherent possibility in being alive, the experience of which depends on one's complete surrender to its realization.

Whether this very brief account of the differences between the different movements of Buddhism, and their approach to the spiritual path and to ordination itself, is accepted or not, the history of Buddhism is undoubtedly largely the history of repeated attempts to communicate the Buddha's vision and the effort to keep that vision alive. The nature of that vision is reflected in the different ways in which dedication to its realization has been expressed. Commitment to spiritual awakening and to treading the Buddhist path to that awakening with and for others is a commitment that has innumerable dimensions; any one formulation of it can never do it full justice.

The Western Buddhist Order is one of the many unfolding forms of Buddhism to arise comparatively recently in the increasingly Westernized world. In terms of traditional Buddhism it is neither a monastic nor a lay order. As the founder of the Order, Sangharakshita, puts it, 'In the Western Buddhist Order one is not ordained as a monk, or as a nun, or as a female probationer, or as a male novice, or as a female novice, or as a male lay devotee, or as a female lay devotee, but simply and solely as a full, practising member of the Sangha or Buddhist Spiritual Community.'[10] The commitment that lies at the heart of this ordination consists in a serious undertaking – whatever the lifestyle of the candidate for ordination (the ordinand) – to follow the transformative path of the Buddha's teachings. Members of the Western Buddhist Order express that determination by going back to the original formula used in early Buddhism, seeing the aspects and developments stressed by the different movements as inherent in this original expression. Within the ordination ceremony the ordinand therefore expresses his or her commitment to the Buddhist path in terms of going for refuge to the Buddha, the Dharma, and the Sangha. It is a commitment to base one's life on the ideals and principles embodied by the Three Jewels and to dedicate oneself to the unfolding dimensions and implications of that key commitment. The many aspects of the Buddhist path are seen as inherent to this essential act of going for refuge, so there is no need for any further or higher ordination in one's quest for Enlightenment. The men and women of the Western Buddhist Order are united by this one essential ordination, whatever their lifestyle, number of years on the path, or choice of practice.

THE IMPORTANCE OF RITES

In this book we will be exploring ordination as a rite of passage. I don't pretend to be familar in any detail with the ordination ceremonies of other religions, or even other Buddhist communities. So to avoid any misrepresentation we will be looking at the ordination that takes place within one tradition and one order, the Buddhist tradition and the Western Buddhist Order. However, the commitment at the heart of the ordination ceremony by which people enter any Buddhist order (perhaps even any order within any spiritual tradition), if wholeheartedly undertaken, undoubtedly marks a watershed in the lives of all of them. It marks the passing through the portals of the old to a new way of being. As such, I believe, it marks a significant event in today's world. This is not because it has any obvious immediate effect on the mass of humanity. In fact, I might say it is just because it doesn't. The significance of Buddhist ordination as a rite of passage arises from ordinary person's struggle to find meaning in a world almost overcome by materialism, a world in which genuine rites, rites that help men and women in the twenty-first century to realize their true humanity (and to which they can relate meaningfully), are few indeed.

We live in a world of change. That is particularly apparent nowadays. Nothing stays as it is for ever. Conditions alter, so things change. Life itself is characterized by change. In fact, we could say that life is change. All things exist as parts of a vast network of conditions which arise from what already is, and then give rise to what is to come. This is true of a nation, a business, a fashion, or even a book. It is also true of a person, a feeling, an act, and a response. Life is an infinitely prolific interplay of interdependent causes and effects.

A rite of passage is a way of marking change. It is, even, a way of celebrating change – not just any change, but change of a qualitative nature, change of a different order. In particular, it is a way of marking such a change in the individual. Ceremonies to ritualize important transitions in our lives have been held since the dawn of mankind. The major life changes of birth, marriage, and death are all marked in this way even today – and in many societies the transition from child to adult too. Through simple ceremonies, such rites mark the transition from one phase of life, social status, or way of being to another. They make the journey of life more conscious and complete, and they make the change public, part of our individual and collective reality. Through some of these rites we still touch upon the sacredness of life; rites have a power that endows certain watershed moments with the significance they deserve. They have something about them that carries change deep into our being, making it part of who we are and transforming us. They carry change beyond our rational mind so that we may know it in our 'soul'.

Ordination means the formal joining of an order. It is a rite of passage that marks a transition to another way of life. This order is a (usually religious) community in which members live according to certain principles, and perhaps vows, based on the teachings of its founder. The essence of acceptance into a Buddhist order involves the witnessing, by senior members of the order, of the taking up of those principles or vows by the person being ordained. This witnessing, and subsequent acceptance into the order or community, takes place in an established and prescribed way, following a pattern set out by the order – the rite of the ordination ceremony.

It was a Belgian anthropologist called Arnold van Gennep who, in the early twentieth century, first used the term 'rite of passage'.[11] He noted a particular pattern in traditional rites that mark the transition between stages of life. He saw that this pattern has three broad aspects. It begins with separation: the person undergoing the rite is separated from their familiar environment and from their normal role or status in the community. The stage of separation is followed by the transition itself: the person frees themself of their former identity and begins to learn of the new stage or status. As we will see, this is to some extent a period of confusion and purification.

When this is complete, the final stage of the rite is performed. This is the reacceptance into the community of that person in their new identity or status.

A typical example of a rite of passage is that through which boys become men in many traditional societies. At a certain age the youth is taken away from the family and community and undergoes a period of trials and ordeals, often in the company of other youths and under the guidance of mentors. Through these trials and the sometimes painful situations they must endure, each of them begins to learn what it is to be an adult. Once the period of transition is complete, they return to their families as adult members of the community.

Rites of passage generally mark changes that are determined by nature; birth, puberty, and death for example. Or they mark changes of status within society, such as marriage. However, there are some rites of passage that mark not so much the unfolding of nature within the life of an individual as the unfolding of spiritual awareness. Such rites mark, ideally, the transition from a passive acceptance of life to an active understanding of its significance and a life based on a spiritual ideal and spiritual principles. We see at least the glimmer of such a ritual transition in the Christian ceremony of confirmation and the Jewish ceremony of bar mitzvah. Confirmation is the youth's affirmation of the religious beliefs and promises outlined for them as an infant at baptism. Similarly, bar mitzvah marks full entry into the religious life of the Jewish community. Examples from other cultures include the American Indian vision quest in which the youth is sent into the wilderness alone, supposedly returning to the community only when the search for a guardian spirit has been completed.

These traditional spiritual rites of passage often coincide with the transition from childhood to adulthood. In traditional pre-industrial societies this transition did not generally include a prolonged social adolescence. It was more or less instant, taking place in the course of the rite in question. However, the deeper significance of a spiritual rite of passage is probably something that only the mature man or woman can know. The transition to a fully active spiritual life is rarely fully undertaken with the purely social or biological change from childhood to adulthood. In recognition of this there exist within many spiritual traditions further rites through which the mature adult can more consciously engage with a life based on spiritual principles and through which he or she can move forward in the quest for fuller spiritual understanding.

Ordination is an example of such a rite. It is a rite that is generally (though not exclusively) undertaken by someone who is already an adult. The ordination ceremony, in this sense, is perhaps particularly illustrative of mature individual dedication to a spiritual ideal and acceptance into a spiritual community based on that dedication. In the Buddhist tradition the commitment made at the time of ordination is not commitment to a dogmatic truth but a commitment to understanding more deeply the nature of life and death – to understanding the truth of our existence – as pointed out in the

Buddha's teachings. It is a commitment to developing the qualities upheld in the Buddhist tradition, such as love, generosity, stillness, truthfulness, and awareness. It is a commitment to helping others to realize their potential as human beings, to transforming the world we live in so that it more fully supports and encourages the spiritual unfoldment of the individual. Though it is specifically a commitment to Buddhism, it is expressive of a universal wish to understand life and to fulfil our deeper selves – an aspiration shared by many – and of the transition to a life based on the living out of that desire. This conscious undertaking, made not by the child-cum-adult but by the mature adult, to understand and to fulfil the deepest significance of their existence, marks an important turning point in life. It is a central transition on the journey of life, more deeply significant than any other, and perhaps more significant now than ever. Amidst all the hollow triviality of so much of modern life, the bold determination of ordinary men and women to live their lives in awareness of its sacredness surely calls for its own celebratory rites.

2

A HUMAN ASPIRATION

What is the knocking?
What is the knocking at the door in the night?
It is somebody wants to do us harm.
No, no, it is the three strange angels.
Admit them, admit them.[12]

The aspiration that led me to practise Buddhism and be ordained as a member of the Western Buddhist Order is not something exclusively 'Buddhist'. It is, as I have said, an aspiration initially to discover the 'meaning of life', and then to live in accordance with it. As such, it is a human aspiration – a desire that is probably experienced, at least occasionally, by everyone, irrespective of time and place, irrespective of cultural and social conditioning, irrespective of religion.

I was 25 when I was ordained. I am now over 40 and much of my life has been the working out of what I came to see, while still in my early twenties, as life's meaning.

As a young man I came to see the meaning of life in Buddhist terms, that is, as the quest for Enlightenment, and since then I have tried to explore ever more deeply what this involves, and live in accordance with it through practising the teachings of the Buddhist tradition.

On a very fundamental level, I am a Buddhist because it is the Buddhist vision of life that best captures for me the sense of wonder that I experience in being alive and which offers me a way of honouring and entering more fully into the mystery, and the awe and the splendour, of existence. This may sound a little abstract, even a little fanciful, but perhaps we can all recall experiences when the extraordinary fact of our existence has particularly struck us. We might have had this experience while reading a book, seeing a film, or meeting someone who reveals to us that there is more to life than we had thought. We might have had it contemplating the beauty of nature or a work of art. We might have had it when faced with the death of a loved one. Such experiences happen when, prompted by some catalyst, we suddenly realize that we are alive and that we are a part of something beyond our comprehension. We realize, for a moment, that we are part of an ungraspable mystery. I remember as a young boy going fishing with my father, and innocently catching my first fish one cold winter day. With its death I knew that something had happened which I did not understand, something sacred. And I sensed for a moment that life – my life – was a miracle. The only way I could honour that miracle at the time was by silently burying the fish in a shallow hole be-hind the garden shed.

Such moments of awareness can often be accompanied by seeing, however briefly, another way of living, a way more in line with this sense of mystery. We glimpse a greater significance to our lives for a moment, and seem to touch upon something essential within us. They are often encounters with someone or something through which we realize that we could live more deeply. Such experiences can, if we wish, be the harbinger of a new life.

There is a story about such an encounter in the canon of Western mythology. Among the well-known legends, the books of ancient tales, is one about a youth called Perceval. Perceval is, of course, a figure from the English Arthurian legends.[13] His story well illustrates a certain moment, and captures an experience we all have now and again – a brief and often sudden instant when an-other way of life irrupts into our world and we see other possibilities. Whatever the externals of their coming, however they may present themselves in the midst of our varied, hectic lives, there are moments when we can choose to embark on a new life.

PERCEVAL

Young Perceval was his mother's last hope, for his father and brothers had all been killed in battle. Not wanting the same fate to befall her remaining son, she brought him up in total ignorance of the existence of knights. He was allowed no weapons and learned to hunt using only short wooden spears.

One day, while out in the woods with his mother, Perceval saw five wanderers riding noble horses and bearing swords and shields. Before his mother could stop him Perceval had put down his work and was watching them in fascination.

'What are those?' he asked in astonishment.

'Why, they must be angels,' his mother replied, fussing with her apron, and hoping with her words to both satisfy his curiosity and to put an end to it.

'Well, I too will go and become an angel!' he called back as he strode to meet the horsemen.

On seeing the young Perceval one of the men asked him if he had seen a solitary knight passing by.

'And what is a knight?' the young man asked in his innocence.

'Such a one as I,' replied the knight.

Young Perceval, though daunted by this man, grabbed his chance to find out more about these strange angel-knights.

'In that case,' said Perceval thoughtfully, 'I will answer you only if you first answer me.'

So Perceval began to ask questions. He asked them about their saddles, their armour, and the name and purpose of the different arms they bore. And he asked again what a knight was, what they did, and why. Finally satisfied, and having no more questions, he answered the knight's question.

Returning to his mother he told her excitedly, 'They were no angels, mother. They were knights!' upon which the poor woman fainted. After taking her home,

Perceval immediately went and fetched his own rather bony, lowly horse, put a pack on its back for a saddle, and twisted twigs and branches in imitation of the fine trappings he had seen. Then, taking some pointed sticks as his arms, he went to his mother and asked her permission to ride forth and become a knight.

'If you must,' she conceded, 'but make sure you go to the court of Arthur, and nowhere else. There you'll find the best and noblest and kindest of knights. Once you get there, tell the king who your father was and ask him for knighthood.'

So Perceval rode forth, preparing to be a knight as best he could on his sorry horse and carrying his home-made arms, but acting nonetheless upon the aspiration that had been kindled in him through that encounter in the woods.

The story of Perceval is a good example of a meeting that can change someone's life. Through his chance encounter, something was touched off in him. He suddenly knew what he had to do, so he did it.

In my own case such an encounter occurred in my early twenties. It was not as sudden as Perceval's, nor did I respond so immediately, but it still changed my life. On leaving university at 21 I was suddenly forced to start making decisions, forced to be something. I didn't know what I wanted to be, and I still hadn't found the meaning I hoped for in life. It was not all unpleasurable of course, but it was unsatisfactory. I sensed there was a deeper meaning to be found, but I didn't know what it was.

It was my girlfriend who was really keen to go to the Buddhist centre, not me. I had by then decided that any search I might undertake for the meaning of life would have to be done alone. I wasn't very eager to go along to a Buddhist group, but since she didn't want to go on her own I eventually agreed to accompany her. They were presenting an introductory course on Buddhism, one evening a week for a couple of months. At the appointed time we found our way to the local Buddhist centre, a small red brick building set back from a busy road, and we entered self-consciously. The course was about to begin, so we joined the circle of people who had already arrived, and the teacher explained what we were about to do. We were going to be exploring the Buddhist vision of life and death.

During the next couple of months he carefully un-folded before us the meaning of life according to Buddh-ism, and the way to live out that meaning. Most of what he taught I missed, being too full of my own pride and youth and with a mind that struggled to grapple with new concepts. But something got through, and the Bud-dhist's words began to change my life: we can all become Buddhas, we can all become Enlightened, or awake to the true nature of existence. It is the search for this Enlightenment that ultimately gives life its meaning.

After this course I spent the next few years trying to understand the message of the Buddha and trying to practise what I had been taught. It gradually became clear to me that this was what I had been waiting for. Although it had come to me in the form of Buddhism I realized that the vision I had been shown touched upon life's deepest and most universal meaning. This meaning did not belong exclusively to Buddhism, rather, Buddhism belonged to it. Buddhism drew it out and unfolded it. I saw that the tradition I had stumbled upon was a uniquely clear expression of the meaning of existence, and how to live out that meaning.

The term 'Enlightenment', as used in Buddhism, refers to an intuitive oneness with reality, an experience of non-separateness with all that lives and a deep sense of being in harmony with our own true nature. It involves all our being in a fully aware response to life and death. The Buddha awoke to this intuitive understanding of the mystery of existence and tried to communicate it to others, and he taught that it was the quest for this spiritual awakening that gave life its meaning. For that reason he taught a path for those who wished to undertake such a quest themselves. This is what I had stumbled across: the communication of the meaning of life as the quest for Enlightenment, and advice on how to fulfil that meaning from one who had himself done so.

At first irregularly, and then weekly, I attended further classes and courses at the Buddhist centre. I learned basic meditation techniques and slowly established a daily meditation practice. This, along with my contact with the Buddhists, began to have its effect, and helped me to get more of a sense of how I might begin to pursue the quest for Enlightenment. A bit like Perceval, I was acting on a chance encounter. Inspired by the Buddha's teaching and the example of those who practised it, and having that basic human aspiration for meaning at last satisfied, I had begun walking the Buddhist path. Lacking almost any knowledge or skill in the quest for awakening, I must often have seemed a bit like Perceval as he rode along on his bony horse sporting his make-believe weapons. Yet, poorly equipped as I was in the qualities and understanding of those whose example I sought to follow, I began to practise. Like Perceval, I began trying to live in accordance with the meaning I had discovered. With the revelation of the ideal of human Enlightenment, and a clearly laid out path to its realization, my whole world had begun to change. There arose in me a natural desire to rearrange my life around the quest I was undertaking. I had a new scale of values and I began to reassess everything in the light of the discovery I had made.

I had few responsibilities, so it was relatively easy for me to begin the process of changing how I lived. Even so, this was not without its difficulties. I decided to stop living with my girlfriend in order to move into a Buddhist community, and I left my job in order to work in a Buddhist building cooperative. I was 23 and full of longing to give myself over to the quest for Enlightenment. I wanted to live what I had discovered to the full, with all my youthful idealism and vigour. I had been shown the potential that life holds and I wanted to realize it within myself. My ideas of Enlightenment and spiritual growth were supremely naive and I was oblivious to the years of effort that would be involved in making any headway whatsoever, but I was determined to join the tradition

started by the Buddha. Not wanting to let the opportunity slip by, I decided to pledge myself to the Buddhist
path and to be ordained within the Western Buddhist
Order.

3

THE MYTH OF THE QUEST

Few among men are those who go to the Other Shore.
The other (ordinary) people chase up and down this
shore.[14]

Throughout history many people have acted on an aspiration to understand life, gone in search of life's secrets,
embarked on the quest for spiritual awakening. Of
course, the idea of questing for Enlightenment is but one
way of understanding what Buddhism is about. It would
be equally valid to use the image of the individual as a
lotus unfolding to the rays of the 'transcendental'. Similarly we could use the image of an ancient path towards
a lost holy city, curing the sickness of ignorance, returning to one's home, discovering a hidden treasure, or
crossing a river. All these images and more have been
used to conjure up what is involved and 'awaken the
dormant spiritual energies of the disciple not by address-

ing his intellect but by making an appeal to his imagination.'[15]

Nonetheless, the quest is one of the greatest of mankind's myths. The myth of the quest is found again and again throughout the world. Whether it is the quest for spiritual awakening, a sacred icon, buried treasure, knowledge, fame and fortune, or love, the stories move us. They are always stories of people who step outside the known and venture forth into the unknown, where they must embark on trials and adventures, even heroic struggles, before they reach their goal.

By 'myth' I do not mean something untrue but something that has universal significance and touches every one of us. Myth is a kind of inspiration. So much of how we live and what we create is sustained by deep archetypes that act as a medium through which universal principles can pass into our lives. Myth is the timeless and universal import of existence given archetypal form and told in legends. And it is in this sense that we can talk of the quest as one of mankind's greatest and most frequently recurring myths.

The Buddhist tradition can be seen as a tradition of questing. The Buddhist way, the Dharma, is the way of searching for the ultimate truth about life. It is a search for ever greater understanding of the nature of existence, ever greater solidarity with other beings, ever greater harmony with the universe. The Buddha himself called this the 'noble quest'.[16] We look for many things in life, but the Buddha distinguished one such search above all others – the search for spiritual awakening. Consisting as it does in wisdom combined with love for all beings (who, we realize, are essentially of the same mysterious nature as ourselves) Enlightenment is the greatest gift that life holds. The quest for Enlightenment, not just for our own sake but for the sake of others, is therefore considered to be the only truly noble quest.

If the quest for the true nature of existence *is* the true meaning of our lives, and therefore the greatest quest of all, there is one story that is worth telling over and over again. It is the story of a man who undertakes that quest and completes it. The story includes elements common to any quest for awakening. In this story those elements, the basic principles of the quest, are told in images and events that speak to the heart as much as to the head. The story involves our emotions and our imagination. Fact mingles with symbolic imagery to communicate the story of Siddhārtha, the man who became the Buddha.

SIDDHĀRTHA

Queen Māyā dreamed that a white six-tusked elephant entered her side. The Śākyan people, inhabitants of a small kingdom situated mostly in what is now Nepal, were delighted, and prepared for the birth of a child to the ruler of their land.

The baby was a boy, healthy and bright-eyed, so there were great celebrations. An old man, revered for his wisdom and powers of prophecy, on hearing of the birth, decided to visit the royal couple and have a look at this new heir. Asita was his name, and when he saw the boy tears began to run down his weather-wrinkled face. The

gathered Śākyans waited. Did this mean bad fortune
was to befall the boy or the people themselves?

'No, I do not foresee any harm will come to the boy or
to the Śākyans,' said Asita, to the relief of all those present. 'This is no ordinary boy; he will come to be either a
great ruler of many lands or a great sage whose message
will reach many people,' he continued. 'I cry because so
little of my life now remains and I will not live to hear his
teaching.'

The Śākyans were overjoyed by this prophecy, though
the thought of his son becoming a great sage rather than
a great ruler did not please the king.

The child was named Siddhārtha, 'he of magical powers', and he was raised by his maternal aunt, his mother
having died seven days after giving birth. He was later
taught by tutors and elders of the Śākyans, imbibing the
customs and knowledge of his people as well as skills in
such arts as horsemanship and archery. As the years
passed, and his son approached manhood, Śuddhodana
the king could see in him the future ruler who had been
prophesied, for Siddhārtha was of noble character and
stature. But the king was also troubled by the other possibility that Asita had prophesied. That his son should
become a great sage was not what the king had in mind;
he wanted him to become a man of worldly power. So he
gave Siddhārtha beautiful palaces – one for each of the
three Indian seasons, we are told – and the delightful
company of friends and dancing girls to amuse him.

Life was undoubtedly good for the young prince, but
his father noticed his restlessness, as if his life amid the

pleasures of the palaces did not really satisfy him. Siddhārtha would look at his father with eyes that seemed to say, 'Is this it? Is this all there is to life?'

'No, indeed, you can have more! You can become a ruler of many lands, a vast Śākyan empire can be yours!' Even so, the king did not sleep easy. Was it just more that his son wanted? Or was it something completely different?

So the king found Siddhārtha a wife, Yaśodharā, the most beautiful girl in the land, with 'face so fair words cannot paint its spell'. As was the tradition, Siddhārtha had to compete with a number of other suitors. We can assume that he had fallen in love, just as his father had hoped, and showing his prowess with bow, sword, and horse he won her hand. For a while Siddhārtha forgot his restlessness, and Yaśodharā soon became pregnant.

One day, Siddhārtha rode out into the city of Kapilavastu – supposedly for the first time – with his charioteer, Chandaka. As they drove through the streets everything seemed much as normal until his eyes settled on an old man with a hunched back tottering along the muddy street. The sight struck Siddhārtha with tremendous force, and we are told that he beheld old age for the first time. There are indeed such moments when the everyday facts of life seem to hit us afresh, as though they had been unseen until then.

Siddhārtha, we are told, asked his companion who this man was, and what had happened that he should appear so. Chandaka replied, 'Prince, this is just an old man. Many years ago his back was straight and his eyes were bright, but now he has no strength and, as you see, his life flickers within him.'

The young prince was shocked. He suddenly realized that old age would come to all – to Yaśodharā, to his parents, his friends, his people, even to himself. Old age was inescapable. We are told that, upon seeing that it was so, the vanity of his youth entirely left him.

On subsequent occasions Siddhārtha had a similar experience on seeing a sick person and then on seeing a dead body. They struck him with that same force, as though he was seeing them for the first time. And in this way the vanity of his health and of being alive left him too.

Then he met a wanderer. It was one of those chance encounters, similar to Perceval's encounter with the knights, a meeting that was to have a decisive effect on Siddhārtha, for he saw the doorway to another way of life. At that time many people wandered the country searching for the truth, or just for a way to 'heaven'. Siddhārtha had no doubt seen other wanderers, but this particular one made a great impact on him. Suppose he himself were to lead the homeless life? Suppose he were to leave home and family, step outside what was expected of him by his father and Śākyan society, and go in search of truth? Suppose he were to dedicate himself to exploring the nature of existence? Thinking thus, his life seemed suddenly to fill with meaning.

Time crept on and Siddhārtha made plans. The king, suspecting as much, set guards inside the palace with orders to prevent him leaving. Nonetheless, one night the prince ordered Chandaka to bring him his horse, Kaṇṭhaka, and together they stole out of the palace. He was no doubt torn by the sight of the sleeping Yaśodharā and his young son who slept at her side, but life at home was 'crowded and dusty' and he longed for a life that was 'wide open'. The desire to live out some deeper meaning called to him, and he could no longer ignore it. The gods softened the fall of Kaṇṭhaka's hooves and, while the guards slept, they flung open the gates. Siddhārtha and Chandaka left the sleeping palace and set out into the night.

After riding until they came to a stream that marked the boundary of the Śākyan territory, Siddhārtha dismounted. Night was giving over to day as he handed Chandaka his princely jewels with instructions to return them to his father, the king. Then, reaching for his sword, Siddhārtha joyfully cut off his long black hair and threw it to the wind. He told Chandaka to return to the palace with Kaṇṭhaka and tell the king of his decision to become a wanderer in search of truth. We are told that both Chandaka and Kaṇṭhaka wept as they left Siddhārtha there on the edge of the wilderness.

In this way Siddhārtha began his quest. Crossing the stream he set off into an unknown land. He soon met a fellow wanderer, poor and dirty, whom he persuaded without much difficulty to exchange clothes with him. Siddhārtha handed over his fine garments and dressed himself in the wanderer's rags. With that he left behind the last vestiges of his former life and became just another wanderer in search of the truth.

He begged for his food, as was the custom, but his first meal tasted so foul that he vomited. During the early period of his wanderings Siddhārtha lived in turn with two teachers, both of whom had a group of followers. The first taught him how to develop a particularly high meditative state of consciousness. Siddhārtha was soon able to achieve this, so his teacher, with nothing else to teach him, suggested he help teach his other followers. Still not having found what he was searching for, Siddhārtha declined and resumed his wanderings in the forest. He then met a second well-known teacher, who taught him how to develop another, even more elevated, state of consciousness. Again, he achieved this quickly and his teacher suggested he actually take over the leadership of his followers. But Siddhārtha was not to be tempted or satisfied by anything less than the discovery of what he had come to call 'the deathless' – that truth that is eternal, beyond the limits of time and space. Siddhārtha wandered deeper into the forest.

Spending each night at the foot of a tree, fear and dread sometimes arose in him as the wind rustled through the leaves and the sounds of the night startled him. But he learned to let such fear come and go, without giving it undue attention.

Then he began to practise asceticism. Among the seekers of that time were a great many who practised forms of self-torture based on the idea that we have a soul that is somehow contaminated and confined by the body and the senses. Siddhārtha applied himself zealously, wilfully beating down his body and his mind. He held his breath to the point of bursting, exposed his body to un-imaginable extremes, and and all this time he ate almost nothing. As the years passed, his body became emaciated and he was hardly able to stand. He became well known for his practice of asceticism, and a band of five companions gathered around him, waiting to share the fruits of his efforts. But Siddhārtha knew that with much more such asceticism he would be none the wiser regarding the riddle of existence. Instead, he would be dead. This was not the way to awakening.

He began to eat more. His five ascetic companions, who had been hoping that Siddhārtha would find the key to the mystery of existence, were shocked. They left him in disgust, muttering about Siddhārtha's lack of determination.

Once again he was alone. He wandered on, too weak to go very far. One day a cowgirl saw him sitting by a stream and brought him some milk-rice in a bowl. After eating his fill, Siddhārtha threw the bowl into the water. It floated upstream, and he took this as a sign. He remembered a time when, as a young boy, while his father was overseeing a ploughing festival, he wandered off to sit in the shade of a rose-apple tree. There he slipped effortlessly into a mood of great contentment and awareness, in which his heart was wide open and whole, and his mind bright and sharp. With that memory Siddhārtha realized the way forward. Refreshed in body and spirit, he went to the shade of a great pipal tree and, making himself a seat from grass given to him by a grass-cutter, he sat down determined to solve the riddle.

'Flesh may wither away, blood may dry up, but I will not move from this spot until I have discovered the deathless.'

He again entered the state of absorption he had experienced under the rose-apple tree. Developing ever greater concentration and vitality, he became more and more deeply absorbed, such that there finally ensued a great battle.

Māra, the evil one, Lord of Darkness and of all the forces of ignorance, approached the Śākyan. Massed around him was a great army of darkness. At first he tried simply to talk Siddhārtha out of it. Hadn't he done enough? He'd done very well to get so far. Why didn't he just spend his days enjoying the fruits of the blissful states he'd discovered? If he wanted he could probably get quite a following! Anyway, was he really sure it was possible to achieve any greater understanding of life's mystery? Wasn't he just chasing an empty dream? Why didn't he just accept that his quest was impossible and call it a day? There were already creeds and dogmas that said what life was all about. Surely others knew better than he did! But Siddhārtha ignored Māra and went still deeper into his meditation.

So Māra summoned his beautiful, seductive daughters. They offered themselves to Siddhārtha, enticing him with promises of sensual delight, and then they sent one in the form of Yaśodharā, who wept and pleaded with Siddhārtha to return to her in their pleasure palace. But Siddhārtha saw them for the illusions they were and sat on.

Dark clouds drew across the sky and thunder rolled across the heavens. The wrathful hordes of Māra came in terrifying forms hissing words of hatred, pride, and fear. A great frenzy of wrath was let loose upon the earth, all directed at the one solitary figure. They flung fire, rocks, whirlwinds, spears, and arrows at Siddhārtha as he sat beneath the tree – then watched in horror as their weapons turned to flowers that gently fell onto the meditating figure. Defeated, the dark hordes disbanded in chaos and confusion.

So Māra made his final move. 'By what right,' he bellowed, 'do you, Siddhārtha, dare to try to comprehend the great mystery, to achieve the deathless? You are not ready, or worthy, of contemplating such a vision, of reaching such an understanding. Only the very greatest have dared to sit where you now sit, on the *vajrāsana*, the diamond throne at the centre of the universe, from where the truth might be discerned. By what right do you now sit here?'

Touching the earth with the fingers of his right hand Siddhārtha called upon the Earth Goddess to bear witness to his effort and progress, both in this life and in previous lives – the effort that had prepared him for this moment. The Earth Goddess appeared and, bowing before Siddhārtha, assured Māra that he was indeed ready and worthy to sit on the same spot as those who had previously gained spiritual awakening. Finally defeated and utterly despondent, Māra departed.

By now the sun had set, twilight had passed, and Siddhārtha sat beneath a full moon. Such was his concentration and his faith in the quest, that as night rolled on Siddhārtha looked back over his life, in fact over all his previous lives. He looked out over the lives of all beings, past and present, and he finally understood. As the day broke, the morning star low in the stillness of the sky, Siddhārtha awoke to the mystery of existence and became a Buddha.[17]

To live out the quest for awakening and its subsequent realization in such a clear and definite manner is unusual. Siddhārtha gained Enlightenment just six years after he left the palace. Even if we do come to see the meaning of life in terms of a quest for spiritual awakening upon which we choose to embark, most of us will spend the best part of this lifetime, at least, in its pursuit.

Even so, any attempt at spiritual awakening will follow something of the course of Siddhārtha's quest, though it might not be as direct. The story of Siddhārtha describes the essential elements of that quest. It seems that any seeker after true wisdom, Buddhist or not, must undertake all the great phases of the path that Siddhārtha himself undertook. Though we must do so in our own way, we too must play out the essential shift in our lives that each phase in the life of Siddhārtha symbolizes. And we will probably need to do so not once but many times, and ever more fully.

We ourselves will need to leave the palace, not just once but again and again. We ourselves must enter the forest, the great unknown, many times. And we ourselves must be true to our quest and not allow the

achievement of minor goals to satisfy us. Our understanding of the mystery of existence will probably not
happen during a night spent under a tree, but through
momentary sparks and flashes of discovery that gradually build up into the clear light of comprehension. We
may need many, many years to overcome the forces of
ignorance, the great hordes of Māra.

Some of us choose to express the aspiration towards realizing our full potential as human beings by consciously
following in the footsteps of the Buddha.
Fundamentally, that is what being a Buddhist means.
We might say that a Buddhist is a human being who sees
the meaning of life as the quest for spiritual awakening,
acts on that aspiration, and takes the Buddha as their example and guide. The story of Siddhārtha, before he became the Buddha, is the rich and brilliant legend upon
which as Buddhists we model our own quest. It would
be difficult to be a Buddhist and not be moved by his
story and not see reflected in it something of the essence
of our own aspirations.

No one is born a Buddhist. Some people are born into a
Buddhist culture, but the real significance of being a
Buddhist implies a choice by the mature individual. A
Buddhist must consciously choose to search for wisdom
and compassion, and make their own decision, just like
Siddhārtha. For myself, and other members of the West-
ern Buddhist Order, the formal expression of that deci-
sion takes place with ordination.

Having established something of a context, we will
now look more closely at ordination within the Western

Buddhist Order, and explore the different aspects of the ceremony itself as a rite of passage, in order to understand how it ritualistically expresses the different stages of all rites of passage. We will also see how it symbolically plays out the different elements of the universal quest for spiritual awakening as embodied in the story of Siddhārtha – elements that the ordinand will have been living out in their preparation for ordination and will continue to live out afterwards.

I don't intend to describe the ordination ceremony in detail, which might make what is a compelling ceremony, rich in myth and symbolism, appear prosaic. It is more important to enter into the spirit of it, and that spirit is found in a broad appreciation of the significance of its various aspects rather than in the details.

4

LEAVING THE PALACE

But when the dusk begins to creep
From tree to tree, from door to door,
The jungle tiger wakes from sleep
And utters his authentic roar.

It bursts the night and shakes the stars
Till one breaks blazing from the sky;
Then listen! If to meet it soars
Your heart's reverberating cry,

My child, then put aside your fear:
Unbar the door and walk outside!
The real tiger waits you there;
His golden eyes shall be your guide.

And, should he spare you in his wrath,
The world and all the worlds are yours;

And should he leap the jungle path
And clasp you with his bloody jaws,

Then say, as his divine embrace
Destroys the mortal parts of you:
I too am of that royal race
Who do what we are born to do.[18]

The rite of passage called ordination gives expression to
a change in the individual that has been set off not by
biological or social factors but by a shift in consciousness.
It is in this sense that it can be thought of as a *spiritual* rite
of passage. Through an encounter of some kind individuals experience a significant broadening of perspective
and sense the possibility of a new way of being. Above
all, there is a shift in perspective with regard to oneself
and the significance of one's life. When Perceval met the
knights in the wood, he realized that he too could be a
knight; when Siddhārtha saw a wanderer he realized
that he too could search for spiritual understanding.

Such a shift in consciousness would necessarily seem
to take place outside one's normal environment, from
where life can be seen anew. Perceval temporarily left his
mother's protection to speak to the knights in the wood;
Siddhārtha temporarily left his palace and ventured into
the unknown world outside. In my own case, it took
place at a Buddhist centre, a world until then quite alien
to my normal environment.

In Chapter 2 I gave examples of ways in which an important shift in consciousness can take place when

reading a book, watching a film, being in nature, or suffering the death of a loved one. Such experiences take us out of our familiar space or mode of experience. We can all identify such an experience of stepping outside our normal environment and realizing that our world is not the only world, our reality not everyone's reality. This commonly occurs, for example, when we are travelling. Those who have had the good fortune to be able to travel to foreign parts will know the sensation of finding ourselves in unfamiliar surroundings. We experience many things for the first time, or as though for the first time. Thus our response to life is fresher. When travelling with an open mind and a sensitivity to our surroundings, we get a different perspective on things, and can have fruitful reflections about ourselves, seeing other possibilities and new ways of being. We experience ourselves to some extent freed from the habits of our familiar routines, more free to respond to our encounters, and better able to see deeply into things. Travellers often return home changed, and tell tales of their adventures.

This shift in awareness can occur not only when we leave the familiar, but also when the familiar suddenly changes or leaves us. We lose our job, or our partner leaves us, and suddenly our world is a very different place. Strange to say, such difficult experiences can also be accompanied by a sense of freedom and the possibility of a new significance to one's life.

Whether the encounter that leads to this broadening of outlook and freedom from old habits takes place outside our normal environment or not, if we follow through that sense of significance it will inevitably lead us into new territory. Change begins with moving beyond the familiar. As such, the first important element we need to look at in ordination is that of separation from the known, the familiar, the established.

Before doing so, we need to explore more fully this aspect of separation in the quest for spiritual awakening and its place in all rites of passage. We have seen how Perceval left his mother and Siddhārtha left his family and tribe. In many ways these examples give us a clue as to what one in search of spiritual awareness first leaves behind. Mother, father, spouse, child, family, and tribe are all primary elements of the social group. The quest for awakening depends to some extent on a willingness to leave the security and the confines of the social group and to go it alone – at least in spirit, but often quite literally. The commitment needed to complete the quest is the commitment of the maturing individual. It is a decision that has to be made for oneself, whatever others may think.

This aspect of the spiritual quest is known in Buddhism as going forth. Traditionally, what we go forth from is 'home', as a symbol of the social group. To some extent it involves both a literal departure from home (at least temporarily), as in the case of Perceval and Siddhārtha, and a more metaphorical departure. We will look at both of these, under the headings of physical going forth and psychological going forth.

PHYSICAL GOING FORTH

Siddhārtha literally left home not only in the sense of leaving the palace and his family, but also in the wider sense of leaving behind his tribe and his homeland.

It seems that the quest for spiritual awakening inevitably involves a degree of physical separation from the social group, or at least some elements of it. It involves some separation, if only temporarily, from the contexts that maintain the status quo and within which we find it relatively difficult to follow through the shift in awareness we have experienced. Perceval's mother deliberately brought him up in ignorance of knights and their way of life. To be able to follow that way of life Perceval needed to leave his mother. Siddhārtha's father had brought him up in the hope that he would show no interest in the spiritual life, and when he did his father tried to seduce him with the pleasures of palace life and then tried to restrain him by force. To be able to follow the aspiration that had awoken in him through meeting a homeless wanderer, Siddhārtha had to break free of his father and the palace life.

I also felt the need to separate myself from contexts that maintained the status quo and which I felt held me back from following through what had been awoken in me by my contact with Buddhism. Long before I became a Buddhist, I had begun to turn away from some of the expectations of the social group. For a time I joined a spiritual group known at the time as the *sannyasins*, followers of Rajneesh (later known as Osho). I was 19 years old and felt the need to break away somehow from what was expected of me by friends, family, and society as a whole in order to begin to give voice to my aspirations. So the sannyasins gave me a new name and I dyed my clothes orange (as was their custom). I even dyed my hair orange. Though this statement of my intention not to live life as others expected might have seemed extreme, it was nonetheless very liberating. It was a breaking of the status quo so as to make of my life something new.

By the time I became a Buddhist I did not feel the need to make such a forceful statement again, though I still felt I needed to free myself from the established way of things. At that time this status quo was represented by life with my girlfriend and my job. Neither of these in themselves prevented me following the Buddhist path. My girlfriend was in fact quite supportive of my desire to practise Buddhism, and interested in doing so herself. Rather it was the act of living as a couple and all that that implied that represented the status quo. And my occupation – a picture-framer running a low cost, fast-service shop – though not actively supporting my aspirations, was in no way detrimental. But against these two aspects of my life stood more radical options: on the one hand, the possibility of living in a Buddhist community of men who had all decided to live the Buddhist path as fully as possible; on the other, the possibility of working with other Buddhists in a small building business run on Buddhist ideals and principles. To refuse either would, at the time, have felt like a betrayal of my aspirations and – despite all that was positive in both my relationship and my job – a denial of my deep-seated response to the Buddhist vision. Though my decision to stop living with my girlfriend and to leave my job was incomprehensible to many, and certainly painful both for her and for me, I felt I had no choice if I was to be loyal to myself. As Jung said, 'A career, producing of children, are all *maya* [illusion] compared with that one thing, that your life is meaningful.'[19]

The important point is that undertaking the quest for spiritual awakening does seem to necessitate some physical separation from whatever it is (not necessarily one's partner or one's job) that maintains the status quo and holds one back from change and growth. Furthermore, this separation is often painful. As James Hollis, a Jungian psychoanalyst, puts it, in talking about traditional rites of passage from childhood to adulthood,

> The abruptness, even violence, of the separation, was a reminder that no youth would voluntarily relinquish the comforts of the hearth. Its warmth, protection and nourishment create an enormous gravitational pull. To remain by the hearth, literally or figuratively, is to remain a child and to forswear one's potential as an adult.[20]

This separation involves leaving behind, at least for a while, everything associated with the old way of being. It is this separation that allows the transition to take place. We have seen that Arnold van Gennep observed that rites of passage generally involve an aspect of physical separation, which means leaving the community or even being removed by force. Rites of passage that mark the transition to adulthood, for example, often involve the child being taken away from its family.[21] In the American Indian tradition of the vision quest, the youth is sent into the wilderness alone. In the rite of passage of marriage, the bride is sometimes separated from her family before the marriage, after which comes the honeymoon, which the couple spend away from family and friends and during which, traditionally, the marriage is consummated. Birth and death include obvious separations: one from the safety of the womb, the other from the known world. Without this separation from what has been, there can be no transition to what is to come.

The social group is made up of a dynamic of established relations, social roles, and behaviour. It is a dynamic based on a common set of beliefs and ideas. For someone to make a shift to a new stage of life, social status, or way of being, they must to some extent step outside this established dynamic. This is normally only achieved by some degree of physical separation. The mature adult who wishes to reorientate their life towards spiritual awakening must to some extent physically leave the social group in order to establish themselves on the spiritual path.

PSYCHOLOGICAL GOING FORTH

Though a degree of physical separation is required, it is fundamentally a psychological separation that takes place. It is in this metaphorical sense that we talk of going forth from home. The aspect of going forth that allows for the transition is essentially an internal leaving behind, even though some external expression will probably be required in order to bring this about. This is particularly true regarding the quest for spiritual awakening. Going forth is above all else an ongoing shift in our attitude towards our self and our world.

If we look at our own lives and the lives of those around us, we can probably see that we all seek self-identity through external factors. We seek an identity in different things, be it our profession, money, sex, partner, family, friends, status, fame, outer appearance, ideas.… The list is endless. We all have things that form the foundations of our life and through which we gain a sense of security and identity. These things – these activities and people – are our point of reference, our refuge, in the midst of life. Through them we maintain a way of being, we feel at *home* with them, and they are well symbolized by that word.

Such self-identification forms part of a healthy and mature response to life. It is through this that we develop a sense of who we are and our place in the world. The disadvantage is that we can come to define ourselves too rigidly through external factors and end up living our lives too fixedly. For example, if we are not careful, we close our life down by identifying it, and ourselves, too intimately with our job or with our partner.

To discover the nature of life and death – the nature of who we are – we have to be able gradually to loosen up the way we see ourselves. This means changing our attitude to things through which we form our self-identity and freeing ourselves from our dependence upon them. This means relying less for a sense of who we are on our profession, money, sex, partner, family, friends, status, fame, outer appearance, or ideas, appreciating and enjoying them for what they are, but not seeking in them (or burdening them with) a sense of who *we* are.

It is this fundamental shift in attitude that is represented, and to some extent facilitated, by the aspect of separation during a rite of passage. The youth must give up relating to the community as a child, just as the members of the community must give up relating to them in the same way, or else forswear the potential to be an adult. Only on that basis the individual can take up the social responsibilities and behaviour of an adult. The single person must give up dependence on parents, or the freedom that being single allows, or forsake fully entering the phase of marriage and raising children. Similarly, though I think it has more far-reaching consequences, the person who is ordained in the Buddhist tradition must give up their fixed way of identifying themselves through external activities, possessions, and other people, in order to embark on the quest to understand who they really are and their true nature. In the Buddhist tradition this giving up is the ongoing process of going forth.

Siddhārtha described life at home as 'crowded and dusty' and yearned for a life that was 'wide open'. It was this same yearning that led Perceval on his adventures. And it was this same yearning that led me, as a young man, to stop living with my girlfriend, quit my job, and seek ordination.

GOING FORTH AT ORDINATION

As a rite of passage, ordination necessarily entails an aspect of separation, representative of the aspect of going forth and individual commitment independent of the social group. In the Western Buddhist Order, this aspect of the rite of passage, and of the spiritual quest, is given expression in various ways.

Within the Western Buddhist Order ordination is marked by a private and a public ordination ceremony. In Chapter 1 I described my own private ordination. This ceremony involves only the person being ordained and the person conducting the ceremony, the private preceptor. The private preceptor witnesses the ordinand's dedication to the spiritual quest and willingness to go it alone, and the private ordination ceremony highlights the fact that it is an individual decision: the mature individual is prepared to make their commitment to the Buddha, the Dharma, and the Sangha whether or not anyone else does so. They are willing to go forth from the social group in order to live out their aspirations, whether or not they have the company of others, and whether or not they have the approval of members of their social group.

This willingness to go it alone, and take complete responsibility for one's commitment, is not only enacted during the private ordination but is given expression in both the private and the public ordination ceremonies through an explicit request for ordination. Though the . actual request will have been made a long time beforehand, the person wishing to be ordained repeats the request during the ceremony using a traditional for-mula. Ordination can only be undertaken as an individ-ual decision, which is made manifest by the ritualized petition.

Though physical and psychological going forth are processes that begin well before ordination, the private and public ordination ceremonies further stress this as-pect of the rite of passage, and the quest for Enlighten-ment, by holding them in the context of a retreat. This takes place during a period of days, weeks, or months during which the ordinands remove themselves from their everyday lives and enter more deeply into contact with their aspirations and their Buddhist practice. Ideally they have no contact with the world they have left behind during the retreat. They receive no news of the world, and the world receives no news of them. Depending on the flavour of the retreat, and the temper-ament of the ordinand, there may be further symbolic acts of this separation and going forth, such as shaving one's head and wearing ceremonial robes instead of one's usual clothes.

The aspect of going forth is further typically intensified in the immediate build-up to the private ordination cere-mony. The ordinands may recount their lives to others, particularly with a view to unburdening themselves of anything that weighs on their conscience. The retreat will then typically move into a period of silence and meditation, during which the ordinands to some extent separate themselves even from each other and reflect on the step they are about to take. In particular, they might meditate on the six elements. Contemplating the six great primary elements of earth (representing all that is solid), water (all that is fluid), fire (the element of heat), air, space, and consciousness, the ordinands reflect that each of these elements exists both within them and within the universe. The individual and the universe are not distinct, and the elements that make up the body and sense of self are the same elements that make up the universe. As such, they do not belong to oneself; they come from the universe and must be returned. In this way the ordinands gradually work on freeing themselves from an over-identification with the material body of earth, water, fire, and air. Similarly they no longer over-identify with the space they occupy, nor limit consciousness to a literalized and polarized experience of self as opposed to other. Through this meditation a kind of spiritual death and sense of freedom occur. In the words of the great Buddhist poet-monk, Śāntideva, one begins to realize that:

> If a (truly existent) [independent] self existed, it would be justifiable to be afraid of any object at all, but since such a self does not exist, who is there to become afraid? Teeth, hair and nails are not the self, the self is not the bones nor blood; it is neither mucus nor is it phlegm; nor is it lymph or pus. The self is not fat nor sweat; the lungs and liver also are not the self; neither are any of the other inner organs; nor is the self excrement or urine. Flesh and skin are not the self, warmth and energy-winds are not the self; neither are bodily cavities the self; and at no time are the six types of consciousness the self.[22]

The sense of a fixed, self-existent self is dissolved, or at least loosened, as the meditator gives up the elements of earth, water, fire, air, space, and consciousness, which are normally identified as 'self', to those same elements in the universe. There arises some understanding that the ongoing, seemingly unchanging experience of an ultimately separate self, with all its associated fears and anxieties, is in fact a misconstruction; that this self is really a seamless process of universal elements and conditions, arising and falling away in ceaseless interplay. Then, perhaps, the greatest going forth of all takes place: the giving up of the very idea of self and other.

5

ENTERING THE FOREST

So now I will go,
I will go on into the struggle,
This is to my mind delight;
This is where my mind finds bliss.[23]

When we free ourselves from whatever holds us back, and act on our aspirations as individuals, we experience a certain happiness. A lightness of heart comes about when we give up what we experience as crowded and dusty, limited or constraining. Of course, there can be sadness or melancholy on saying goodbye to things we have known for so long, but there is also an undeniable joy. We sense it in the story of Perceval as he fetches his horse and asks his mother for permission to ride forth, and we sense it in the story of Siddhārtha as he rides with Chandaka through the night. It is the joy of acting upon a greater awareness: the recognition of a higher possibility and the aspiration to live it out.

This going forth takes us into unknown territory. Perceval sets off into the vast forests to wander in search of adventure; Siddhārtha crosses the river marking the boundary of his territory and sets off in search of the deathless. Their quest for the unknown takes place in an unfamiliar land. To find the unknown they must enter the unknown, just as the young American Indian must enter the wilderness to meet with the guardian spirit.

My own quest has certainly led me into unknown territory, quite literally: from the relative strangeness of a Buddhist community to more recent homeless years teaching the Dharma on both sides of the Atlantic, and from the inspired naivety of attempts to establish a co-operative building business along Buddhist principles to the equally inspired naivety of leaving my homeland and founding a Buddhist centre on the Mediterranean coast of Spain.

Whatever its form, literal or metaphorical, it is in this wilderness that the individual must learn *how* to quest. It is a period of purification and preparation for an encounter with that which they seek. It is often a period of confusion, disorientation, and even humiliation. And it is usually the longest phase of a rite of passage.

CONFUSION AND HUMILIATION
Perceval sets off on his adventures only to become known as a fool. He suffers many defeats and misadventures before he comes to the Grail Castle and the Fisher King, whereupon his foolishness only grows. The Fisher King, also known as the Grail King or the Wounded King, is the guardian of the Holy Grail. As a wounded king his

powers have been weakened, and his land, surrounding the Grail Castle, has become a wasteland. At the same time he is also seen as the grand black magician of the Underworld. He is called the Fisher King because he once fed many people from a single fish, though the name is also thought to be a play on the French word for 'sinner' (*pecheur*). The Fisher King is a figure of confusion and in need of healing. It is on meeting the Fisher King that Perceval's greatest humiliation takes place.

On his arrival at the castle, Perceval finds the Wounded King and sees both the Holy Grail and the Sacred Spear pass by in a procession. It is said that those on the quest will see these sacred objects, and on so doing must ask the Grail Question, which will both heal the Wounded King and restore the Wasteland. The question concerns the purpose of the quest and what it will mean, but Perceval fails to ask the all-important question. It is this failure that is the source of his humiliation before Arthur's knights. Perceval must then undergo a further series of trials and adventures in order to purify himself before he is able to return to the Grail Castle and heal the Wounded King.

Siddhārtha, too, falls into some confusion. His disorientation on entering foreign lands is hinted at in his inability to keep down the food he is given and the fear he experiences at night. He spends time with two different teachers, and takes up the severe practice of asceticism in the company of misguided friends, before he discovers the way forward. His practice of asceticism brings him close to death, and after his Enlightenment he denounces it as not forming part of the spiritual quest.

My own experience of treading the Buddhist path has also entailed confusion and humiliation, as I have sought to understand what I am doing and where I am going. When I first moved to Valencia to set up a Buddhist centre I naively believed it would take only six months, after which I would be ready to dash off and set up other centres all over Spain. In fact I spent nine years working with friends to establish what is still a relatively small centre in Valencia. During the course of those years I had to cope with many difficulties and made many mistakes. I struggled to deal with my own cultural conditionings in a foreign land and was forced to face up to my limitations in communication and leadership. I had to accept that my spiritual quest was not going to take place in a blaze and a final flash of glory, but that it was going to be a much more discreet and everyday affair. I had to learn to open up to a deeper appreciation of the Buddhist path and teachings and I experienced humiliation when I was unable to put my ideals and principles into practice; when other desires and motives triumphed. Questions, uncertainties, and doubts are common companions in the quest for spiritual maturity and there are moments in my life as a Buddhist when I have wondered whether I am up to the task I have set myself.

PURIFICATION

In a well-known passage from the Buddhist scriptures the purified mind is likened to a white cloth.[24] Just as the white cloth instantly takes up the colour of dye, so the purified mind takes up the truth of the Dharma. To be able to realize their goals, both Perceval and Siddhārtha had first to prepare themselves. They had to purify themselves of all that prevented them seeing the way forward. Their minds and hearts had to be able to hold what they sought. A process of purification is necessary in order to realize a transition to a new way of being. The transition from an old way of being to a new inevitably consists in first having to prepare oneself. It means making mistakes and getting it wrong until one is free of everything that hinders the transformation.

We see this aspect of purification in nearly all rites of passage. It is an essential aspect of the phase of transition. The rite of passage that marks birth and the acceptance of the child into the Christian community, for example, involves immersion in holy water; ceremonies marking the transition from boyhood to manhood often involve circumcision; the bride in many cultures wears white. So as to make the transition from the old life to the new, or from the old social status to the new, the individual must first be purified of the old. The baby's soul must be purified in order to enter the Christian community; to become a man the boy must be purified and tested; the young woman must be a virgin – symbolically at least – in order to be able to consummate the marriage in a state of purity.

This process of purification is also present in one's progression towards ordination. It begins some time, usually several years, before the ordination itself. It begins the moment someone requests ordination. With that

request they enter unknown territory and begin to prepare their heart and mind in order to maintain the commitment they are later to make. The preparation for
ordination involves study and practice and the development of strong links of friendship with members of the
Order. This period of training is a time during which the
ordinand deepens their understanding of the Buddhist
path and the nature of the Order. It is a period during
which they will face many questions and doubts, come
to know themselves and their motives more deeply, get
to know members of the Order more fully, and struggle
with the implications of the path they wish to tread. It is a
period during which many of their assumptions about
life will be challenged. Although this preparation is a period in which horizons open, it is also a journey marked
by hazards, and though it offers a means of realizing
more fully those aspirations on which it is based, it offers
no promise of completion. Above all, like other phases of
transition, it involves dealing with the confusions and
humiliations of trying to become someone new – before
the joys of that transition can be fully experienced.

In the ordination ceremony itself ritual purification
takes place in several ways. At the beginning of the ceremony the ordinand recites verses of purification expressive of their preparation and the purification that will
continue throughout their quest: 'Bowing before the
Buddha, I purify my body; chanting the sacred mantras,
I purify my speech; silently meditating, I purify my
mind.' Later, the preceptor pours a small amount of con-
secrated water, a universal symbol of purification and

bestower of life, onto the crown of the ordinand's head. On the basis of this purification, the person being ordained undertakes a set of ethical precepts through which body, speech, and mind are to be further purified. Finally, they accept the white kesa, a narrow strip of cloth emblazoned with the image of the Three Jewels, which may be worn around the neck as a symbolic 'robe' of the Western Buddhist Order. The presentation of the kesa marks full acceptance into the Order. As the scriptures say, it is only the white cloth that takes instantly the colours of a dye, only the purified mind that takes the truth of the Dharma.

Because of the importance of purification in the quest for spiritual awakening, and of its symbolic representation within the ceremony, we are going to look at it more closely, especially as it manifests in training for membership of the Western Buddhist Order. One way of understanding this period of preparation and purification is through looking at the basis on which the ordinand finally accepts ordination. During the ceremony, the new Order member explicitly accepts ordination and expresses the spirit in which the quest for the goal of Enlightenment is to be lived out. Being able to accept ordination in the spirit it deserves means first purifying oneself, at least to some extent, of other motivations. This purity of motivation is expressed through the acceptance of ordination on four counts: loyalty, harmony, for the sake of Enlightenment, and altruism.

LOYALTY

Firstly, ordination is accepted in a spirit of loyalty to one's teachers. In many rites of passage the role of a guiding figure is central. Such a figure can take many guises: the mentor who shows the way to adulthood, the priest who exhorts the married couple, even the midwife who delivers the baby. In many traditions a benign spirit guides the soul or consciousness of the deceased in the afterlife. In the spiritual quest this guiding figure is most commonly thought of as one's teacher. For that guiding figure to oversee the transition from the old to the new it is necessary for the ordinand to trust their teacher and be loyal to them.

A teacher is someone who helps others to learn, who tells or shows them how to do something. Within Buddhism a teacher is someone who reveals the Dharma and shows others how to practise it. As such, the first and greatest teacher is the Buddha himself. Being an ecumenical order, open to the entire Buddhist tradition, members of the Order also view many other great Buddhist figures as teachers,[25] and individual Order members often receive particular inspiration from specific historical teachers. Sangarakshita is our most immediate teacher, having clarified the basic principles of the Dharma and appropriate means by which to practise them in the world today.

Within Buddhism it is common to talk of one's teachers as spiritual friends (*kalyāṇa mitras*). Teachers are friends who help one along the path of the Dharma. Seeing one's teachers in this way enables a healthier relationship to develop between teacher and disciple, and places it within a wider context of multiple friendships and relationships. One's teachers are not one's only spiritual friends, and companions in the spiritual life are also seen as sources of inspiration, support, and guidance from whom one can learn. Of particular importance in the ordination ceremony are the preceptors who oversee the private and the public ordination ceremonies.[26] It is the preceptors who are ultimately responsible for guiding the ordinand through the process of becoming a member of the Order, and it is the preceptors who witness the commitment made at the time of ordination. It is from these preceptors that the ordinand takes the ethical precepts that will lead them towards awakening, and it is these preceptors who, ideally, will act as guides throughout the years ahead. For this to be possible the ordinand needs to be open to the greater experience of these spiritual friends and maintain confidence in them.

This ability to be loyal is of great importance. While the quest for awakening can only be undertaken by the individual, he or she must nonetheless be able to trust in others with more experience. None of us can make progress in spiritual understanding without a helping hand, and it is the attitude of loyalty that keeps us in relationship to those who can guide us.

Loyalty to one's teachers means being faithful to them and their teaching. Though it inevitably means attending to and following their exposition of the Dharma, even following their advice, it means above all being faithful to that same spirit with which they lead the quest for awakening. It means following their example. It is highly unlikely that one's own teachers will be free from faults and imperfections, and they will probably have made mistakes in their quest. In fact, an important aspect of purification on the path to ordination, indeed to spiritual awakening itself, involves developing a less naive, and therefore more mature, appreciation of what spiritual development entails. Treading the Buddhist path often seems to require coming to terms with imperfections and contradictions within those one sees as one's teachers. The story of Buddhism in the West seems to reflect this; the story of the Western Buddhist Order certainly does. Some Order members have had to come to terms with what they see as contradictions in the life of the founder of the Order, Sangharakshita, and with their own and others' shortcomings in acting as preceptors and spiritual friends. Loyalty does not mean following the example of one's teachers in all that they do and say. In fact, to do so may at times be an act of disloyalty if things they have said or done go against our conscience or against the Dharma.

This sense of loyalty to one's teachers, and the commitment to the Three Jewels that they exemplify, is given expression in two well-known verses by Śāntideva:

Today my life has (borne) fruit;
(Having) well obtained this human existence,
I've been born in the family of [the] Buddha
And now am one of [the] Buddha's Sons.

Thus whatever actions I do from now on
Must be in accord with the family.
Never shall I disgrace or pollute
This noble and unsullied race.[27]

Someone who becomes a member of the Western Buddhist Order does so because they believe Buddhism, as a spiritual tradition, to be the best way to spiritual awakening, and the Western Buddhist Order the context in which they wish to practise it. They do so in part because they see that at the heart of the Order lies genuine commitment to this spiritual awakening, and because they see that what motivates their spiritual friends, preceptors, and teachers is that same aspiration and dedication on which they wish to base their own lives. One is loyal to one's teachers as exemplars of this aspiration, despite their contradictions, imperfections, and mistakes – perhaps even because of them.

To reach such a point necessarily involves a process of clarification and motivation. Apart from the unrealistic (if understandable) desire to see perfection in others, another common motivation that many people have to purify is the desire for acceptance from those we see as our teachers. Though it is natural to want the approval of those whose example we follow, we may find ourselves following the advice of spiritual friends not because we want to deepen the aspiration and commitment we see reflected in them, but because we have an unhealthy need for acceptance from those we think are in a position of authority. Similarly, some may have to work to overcome an equally neurotic inability to really trust and be open to others, in this case those who have more experience of the spiritual path and who are therefore in a position to help and guide.

It is only by having purified such motivations that we can, as mature individuals, start to practise loyalty to our spiritual friends. Having chosen our context we need to be loyal to it if it is to work, sticking with it and with our friends. Such loyalty is an expression of our individual working out of the universal quest for spiritual awakening; we see that to be loyal to our teachers, and the spirit of the quest they embody, is to be loyal to our own human aspiration to awaken.

HARMONY

Ordination is also accepted in harmony with other members of the Order. Accepting ordination means taking on the challenge of realizing the true nature of the Order as a spiritual community or sangha. In the arts, harmony is the effect produced by the pleasing arrangement of forms, sounds, or colours. In the spiritual community, it is the effect produced by individuals coming together on the basis of shared aspirations and commitment, a coming together that is not only pleasing but also deeply significant and emotionally rewarding. With harmony there is concord, a word that derives from the Latin *com+cor* meaning 'same heart' or 'of one heart'. 'Of one heart' well describes the experience of friendship in the spiritual quest.

Someone joining the Order must be able to base themself upon this shared aspiration and understanding in their relationships with others, having an attitude of friendship and good will towards those with whom they make up the Order. In practice, the ability to hold such an attitude means cultivating the ability to go beyond likes and dislikes and being able to relate to a very diverse collection of people on the basis of a shared allegiance to the Three Jewels. It means working to free ourselves of prejudices of race, nationality, sex, class, and politics. It means being able to disagree with ideas without losing an underlying empathy with those who hold those ideas. It means entering into full dialogue with others while studying and exploring the Buddhist path with them in a shared attempt to arrive at a deeper understanding. It means being able to tread the Buddhist path with others who are attracted by often very different aspects of this diverse tradition. It is only those who have freed themselves from an over-identification with their own conditionings, likes, and dislikes who are able to begin to do so. To reach such a stage of freedom and sense of harmony involves purifying ourselves of any obvious attachments and prejudices, and at the same time becoming much clearer about our thoughts and values. Both discord and conformity are the enemies of harmony.

It is important, therefore, that someone who wants to become part of the Western Buddhist Order understands that it aspires to be a true sangha in the deepest sense of the word, and that they are able to take on such a commitment. It means making sure that they realize that the Order is not just another ecclesiastical organization, faction, or group of which one is a member by dint of following certain rules, attending certain meetings, or putting one's name to certain beliefs. The Order is a community of people bound together by a common ideal, each having made their personal commitment to that shared ideal, the ideal of spiritual awakening. The coming together of people who have all, independently, made the decision to realize life's meaning, and whose perception of that meaning and the means to its realization coincide, is a unique experience. It is a gathering of individuals who have made their own journeys and their own decisions and commitments. Not surprisingly, a special friendship often arises between them. They find themselves with others who base their lives on those same aspirations and tread the same path. Even without the blossoming of friendship they often form strong links through a mutual recognition of their common humanity and shared dreams. Because of what they have all chosen to do with their lives, such free individuals are able to appreciate the significance of that choice in each other.

Of course, any free association of individuals is always in danger of quickly becoming yet another group, and this is as true of the Western Buddhist Order as of any 'religious' community. It is for this reason, in part, that an understanding of sangha is emphasized during preparation for ordination.

A group, at its worst, is a collective in which the interests of that collective override the interests of the individual. For a group to be a group, all its members must conform to its norms, and most of those who make up the group will not deviate from those norms (or, as it were, think for themselves), for fear of losing the acceptance of others in the group. Likewise, they will tend to coerce and manipulate others to accept the values, outlook, and behaviour of the group. The primary relation of those involved in such a group is to the group itself, rather than the individuals who constitute it. Though the most extreme examples of this sort of dynamic may be found in, for example, religious sects and political parties, this negative group dynamic is often to be found in one form or another in many other walks of life. Elements of such a dynamic can appear within families, in the workplace, or between friends. Within any spiritual community there is the constant danger that such a dynamic will occur, and it has almost certainly sometimes occurred within the Western Buddhist Order. There have been occasions on which members of the Order have (usually unwittingly) put psychological pressure on others to conform to specific ways and beliefs.

As we have seen, the Order aspires to be a sangha rather than a group.[28] Just as an individual needs to pass through a process of purification in their quest for spiritual maturity, so too a collective that strives to embody true sangha must constantly purify itself of anything that prevents it being so. Sangha is a free association of all those who aspire to ever-greater awareness of the mysterious nature of existence, both in themselves and in others. Those who have fully established themselves in this intuitive understanding of the nature of existence will naturally relate to others on the basis of this awareness, and it is this that creates *ārya* or noble sangha. What happens in the coming together of such individuals can probably only be imagined or intuited – it is a dimension of consciousness difficult to experience, let alone describe.

Of course, for the Western Buddhist Order to be an expression of *ārya* sangha it is dependent on all its members having this transcendental awareness of reality – which they don't. Members of the Western Buddhist Order are simply devoted to unfolding such an awareness. Membership of the Order says nothing about one's state of spiritual wakefulness. However, the principle of harmony is still central to the Order. The harmony of the sangha at the level of the Order arises not from full realization of the nature of existence, but from commitment to a shared aspiration, from mutual feelings of respect and friendship, and from a common vision of the essential nature of the spiritual path.

FOR THE SAKE OF ENLIGHTENMENT

The third basis for the acceptance of ordination is for the sake of Enlightenment. We have seen how Siddhārtha never allowed other achievements to distract him from his search for the deathless. In particular, he never allowed partial spiritual attainments to satisfy him, nor the onset of fame and prestige. Taking up religious practice can bring many mundane advantages that have nothing to do with spiritual progress. This is perhaps particularly the case if one teaches others, though not exclusively. Flattering attention from students, financial rewards, social status, and the illusion of a greater spiritual maturity than may be the case can take the edge off the spiritual quest, and these have distracted many people from the ultimate goal. It is easy for the ego to hijack our spiritual endeavours, turning our quest into a form of self-aggrandisement, or simply complacency. As my own teacher has written:

> Here we encounter in its acutest form the central problem of the spiritual, as distinct from the merely religious, life. The ego-sense … instead of being eliminated thereby, simply transfers itself to those very practices which were intended to annihilate it. Like an unwanted but faithful dog, it is kicked out of the front door only to creep in at the back. Herein lies the tragedy of many a spiritual life. The more we struggle to eliminate our ego-sense the subtler and stronger and more dangerous it becomes. We revolve within a vicious circle from which there seems to be no possibility of escape. The man who thinks 'I am enlightened' is equally far from Nirvana as the man who thinks 'I am rich'. The saint may be more attached to his sanctity than the sinner to his sin.[29]

Individuals within the Western Buddhist Order and elsewhere run the risk of losing sight of the true reason for spiritual practice and entering a spiritual community. The only valid reason and goal is that of awakening or Enlightenment. As part of an order and an international Buddhist movement it might be easy to find oneself distracted by such matters as status and position, financial security, or worldly satisfaction in running a Buddhist movement, and it is with an appreciation of these dangers, and others, that the person being ordained explicitly accepts their ordination for the sake of the attainment of Enlightenment, not the attainment of anything else. Once again, to have reached the point of being able to accept ordination in such a spirit, they will first have had to purify themselves, to some extent, of these other motivations for seeking ordination. Having accepted ordination on this basis, all Order members find themselves obliged to face up to and purify the mixed motives that inevitably appropriate the endeavours of a spiritual life.

ALTRUISM

Finally, ordination into the Western Buddhist Order is accepted in a spirit of altruism. It is accepted for the benefit of all beings. As Śāntideva wrote, many centuries ago, in relation to the Bodhisattva:

> *This intention to benefit all beings,…*
> *Is an extraordinary jewel of the mind,*
> *And its birth is an unprecedented wonder.*[30]

Rites of passage are often undertaken for the benefit not only of the individual, but also the wider community. The youth becomes an adult in order to take up new responsibilities, in part so that the wider community can continue. Similarly, ordination, and the commitment to the Three Jewels at the heart of this rite of passage, is not an isolated, 'personal' act but something that takes place within the context of one's connectedness to all living beings. Our lives are tied up with the lives of others, and it would be impossible to truly take up the ideal of the

Buddha without a keen awareness of and sensitivity to the joys and sufferings of those around us, as well as a desire to help them become happier and more fulfilled. Those who undergo the transition to membership of the Western Buddhist Order do so not just for their own sake but because of a conviction that this is how they can best help others.

Spiritual practitioners are sometimes portrayed as 'contemplating their own navel', and it is true that it is easy to become self-obsessed in the search for one's 'own true nature'. Yet such an awakening in fact requires a greater awareness of others and the world we inhabit, as well as a strengthening of our sense of interconnected-ness with all. To be able to accept ordination into the Western Buddhist Order not just for one's own well-being but for the sake of all beings requires purifying oneself, at least to some degree, of a self-centred percep-tion of one's own life and seeing that one's actions have implications for the wider community – and ultimately for the whole world. The going forth, so essential to the spiritual quest, is not a haughty looking away from the world but an attempt to gain a fresher, larger, and more deeply penetrating perspective on one's own existence, not least so as to contribute more positively to life on this planet. The Buddha himself seems continually to have encouraged his followers to develop good will and loving kindness towards others.

> Even as a mother, as long as she doth live, watches over her child, her only child, – even so should one practise an all-embracing mind unto all beings.[31]

Accepting ordination in this spirit of altruism means learning to tread the spiritual path while maintaining a healthy tension between two pulls: the pull towards self-awakening and the alleviation of one's own suffering, and the pull towards helping others to overcome their suffering through awakening. This tension will often manifest as a conflict in what one does with one's limited time and energy, between meeting one's own needs and those of friends and family. Without this tension there is a fruitless escape into navel gazing and spiritualized self-obsession on the one hand, and a confused anxiety-driven attempt to patch up the woes of the world and do-goodery on the other. Wisdom and compassion go hand in hand: there is no true wisdom without compassion, no real compassion without wisdom. Ordination within the Western Buddhist Order is accepted for the sake of Enlightenment, and at the same time for the benefit of all beings, and it is from the tension experienced by keeping these two aspects alive in one's life that real transformation comes about, for 'liberation is not so much of the self as from the self'.[32] In this way, the Bodhisattva, or one who strives to attain Enlightenment and helps all beings to do likewise,

> looks both within and without. External activities do not for him preclude internal calm and recollection, neither do his indefatigable exertions on behalf of all sentient beings prevent him from enjoying uninterruptedly perfect peace of mind.[33]

Through living out one's ordination for the benefit of all beings the crude tension between self and other is gradually purified and gives way to a liberating sense of mutuality within which one's own life and the lives of others merge naturally one into the other. There gradually arises an experience of the ultimate emptiness of any real distinction between the two.

When someone is accepted into the Order it is because those responsible for conducting the ordination have seen that this process of purification – as expressed in these four ways – has taken place sufficiently for the individual to be ready to undergo the transition to the new, that they are ready to begin a new phase of their life because they have in fact already embarked on a new way of being. However, this does not mean that the process of purification is over. The path to Enlightenment to which the new Order member is committed requires that this purification be continued long after ordination, indeed throughout the whole quest for spiritual awakening.

6

BENEATH THE TREE OF KNOWLEDGE

Shri Ri, that wondrous place in Jal,
Is far to circle, but near to approach.
Come here, you faithful and destined devotees
And all who would renounce this world and life.

Here is the wonderland, Shri Ri,
Far indeed from towns,
But close to meditation and accomplishment!
Come to Shri Ri, you faithful and destined devotees
And all who would renounce this world and life! [34]

The story of a quest that takes the hero on a distant journey, only to discover that what they seek has always been close to hand, recurs in various spiritual traditions. The Buddhist tradition tells the story of a young man who, believing himself to be destitute, travels to a distant country and endures many struggles before discovering that he carries a precious gem sewn into the lining of his coat.[35]

The message of such stories is clear. The true nature of existence which we seek to discover through the spiritual quest is not only of unfathomable beauty and richness, it is also with us all the time; we just don't see it. We first need to go through a process of purification in order to understand.

In the course of the quest for awakening, as we purify our minds and hearts, we come to realize the importance of events that we had previously overlooked. The process of searching that leads Siddhārtha to practise with first one teacher, then another, before taking up asceticism, finally leads him back to his childhood experience under a rose-apple tree. That experience had, in a sense, been with him all the time, but he had not been able to recognize it for what it was. Only by having searched and purified himself for six years was he able to do so.

A process of purification seems always to lead one back to one's own experience, but with eyes that are now clear enough to be able to see it and a heart whole enough to be able to fathom it. Without that process of purification one is not able to hold the ever-present truth.

WHEN THE TIME IS RIGHT

After many adventures and trials Perceval, the 'pure fool', eventually returns to the Grail Castle and heals the Wounded King. Perceval is a figure who appears in many guises throughout retellings of this ancient story. In an early pre-Christian version Perceval (or Peredur, as he is known there), on meeting the Fisher King for the first time, is advised not to ask any questions about anything that happens while he is in the Castle, and once he has left not to tell anyone about what he has seen. We see in this version of the story that it would in fact have been foolish for Perceval to have asked about things that pertained to another realm of being. It would have been foolish to ask before he was capable of understanding the answer. The Fisher King does not give away his knowledge so carelessly. The desire to obtain answers prematurely would have been what designated Perceval a fool. In this other version, we see that Perceval was wise not to ask the Grail Question concerning the purpose of the quest and what it would mean. It was too soon for him to know. He wasn't ready.

In our own lives it is tempting to try to attain goals before we are ready. When we do this it is because we think of the goal as something to *have* rather than a more organic – and fragile – process of change and growth. So many of my own spiritual endeavours have been little more than grasping at the teaching of the Buddha: trying to understand the nature of existence before I sufficiently understood myself, wanting to become a Buddha before becoming a man. In this way there is a premature birth of the new, and what is premature struggles to survive. Perhaps we could do with remembering Rilke's advice to a young poet friend:

> Be patient toward all that is unsolved in your heart and try to love the *questions* themselves.... Do not now seek the answers, which cannot be given you because you would not be able to live them. And the point is, to live every-

thing. *Live* the questions now. Perhaps then you will gradually, without noticing it, live along some distant day into
the answer.[36]

This coming to the answer, or entering the next phase of
change when the time is right, often manifests
mythically as entering a sacred space. The youth of the
vision quest, who goes alone into the wilderness in
search of his guardian spirit, does so after purification in
the sweat lodge. In the wilderness he sits in the centre of
a sacred circle. This is the sacred spot of direct experience, where he has an intimate and direct vision of the
guardian spirit, usually in the form of an animal. This
spirit animal has always been his guardian, without him
knowing it.

Siddhārtha, having passed through a process of purification and finally realized the way forward, sits beneath
the tree which later became known as the bodhi tree, the
tree of Enlightenment. The tree is a universal symbol of
life. Its roots reach deep into the earth and its branches
high into the heavens. The place beneath the bodhi tree
is also a sacred spot, known as the *vajrāsana*, the 'diamond throne'. It is said to be the centre of the universe
and, again, can be thought of as the place of direct experience. It is here that Siddhārtha is able to call upon the
Earth Goddess, witness to his preparation and to his
worthiness to sit on this spot. It is here that he is finally
able, when the time comes, to claim his right to sit in the
place of awakening, from where the Buddhas arise.

This idea of a sacred space is reflected in the ordination
ceremony by creating a special space for it. Statues or

images of the Buddha are enshrined here, perhaps after the ground or room has itself been ritually purified and prepared, and it is in the presence of these that the ordinand makes his or her commitment. It is to this sacred place, symbolic of direct experience, that the ordinand, over time, makes their way. This too is entered only when the time is right.

COMMITMENT

The understanding that has come about through the process of purification allows for a truer and more integral transition within a rite of passage. The transition to the new is more organic, because it is based on some personal experience of what is to come. The central point of this transition is the point of commitment. When this commitment is undertaken at the right moment and in the right place it leads to a natural flowering of the new.

To commitment oneself is to pledge allegiance to what is coming into being; it means giving oneself over to another phase, social position, or way of being. It is the central act in any rite of passage. There comes a moment when the youth actually confirms his or her religious beliefs as an adult; a moment when the married couple actually take the marriage vows; perhaps a moment when the deceased decides to move towards the light. Just as going forth means giving up the old, so commitment means embracing what is to come. Without a point of commitment the transition cannot take place; it forms an essential part of any rite of passage and marks the definitive move towards another way of being. It is the

point at which we identify with the new phase and en-
trust ourselves to it. It has something irrevocable about it.

The words of the Siddhārtha as he sat beneath the
bodhi tree conjure up the determination which is an
aspect of commitment. 'Flesh may wither away, blood
may dry up, but I will not move from this spot until I
have discovered the deathless.' These are not words of
naive, immature heroism. They are words that capture
the moment in which Siddhārtha's whole being begins
to move towards his transformation into a Buddha – just
as the petals of a lotus bud simultaneously begin to unfold. Nonetheless, mature commitment, though based
on conviction and some experience, still requires decision, even heroism, if it is to bear fruit. Transformation
necessarily means moving towards what is still ultimately an unknown. It involves some degree of risk and
some degree of heroism if that transformation is to fulfil
its promise. As Jung says:

> The spirit of evil is fear, negation, the adversary who
> opposes life in its struggle for eternal duration and thwarts
> every great deed.… For the hero, fear is a challenge and a
> task, because only boldness can deliver from fear. And if
> the risk is not taken, the meaning of life is somehow vio-
> lated, and the whole future is condemned to a hopeless
> staleness, to a drab grey lit only by will-o'-the-wisps.[37]

Commitment to the spiritual quest, looked at in
mundane terms and from the point of view of the old
way of being, is not only risky but reckless. When looking at the aspect of separation in rites of passage, and the

fundamental importance that Buddhism assigns to going forth, we saw that in order to enter a new phase of transformation we need to be able to let go of how we identify ourselves in order to move towards a new way of being. We saw earlier that most of us rely for a sense of who we are on such things as our profession, money, sex, partner, family, friends, status, fame, outer appearance, and ideas. These give us a sense of security and even protection against the vicissitudes and difficulties of life, and through them we seek our happiness. We could say that we seek refuge in these things. To give up the sense of security our mundane refuges afford can seem both rash and irresponsible. Yet commitment to the Buddhist path involves a decision to orientate one's life away from reliance on such things and towards the spiritual ideals of the Buddha, the Dharma, and the Sangha. It means going forth from an identification of who, or what, we are based on those things and seeking refuge in ideals, principles, and experience that go altogether beyond time and space. And that needs courage.

COMMITMENT AS A DEEPENING PROCESS
Paradoxically, full commitment to the Three Jewels is only truly realized when one becomes Enlightened. It is only then that one's whole being and life is based fully on spiritual awakening – when one has in fact actually awoken. The commitment made by those who become members of the Western Buddhist Order is a commitment to the process of becoming Enlightened and basing one's life ever more fully on the ideals and principles of the Three Jewels.

Within the Western Buddhist Order we recognize that there are degrees of going for refuge to the Buddha, the Dharma, and the Sangha. In many Buddhist countries people recite verses of commitment to the Three Jewels simply because they have been born into a Buddhist society and it is the normal thing to do. Just as many people in the West are only nominally Christians, having been baptized as a child, many people in the East 'go for refuge' to the Three Jewels. They recite verses of devotion to the Three Jewels in much the same way as many of us have sung hymns. Though there may be devotion and appreciation, which should certainly not be undervalued, there might only be a limited understanding and commitment.

However, a somewhat more critical, and individual, commitment is possible, within which there exists a sense of the ideals embodied in the Three Jewels, and an openness to exploring them and trying to embody them, even though there might not be a wholehearted adoption of them. They are accepted somewhat provisionally and someone becomes dedicated to them in the sense of investigating them further, even though they do not as yet have the understanding or desire to make a decisive commitment.

When that understanding and desire arises the individual is able to make that commitment more decisive. It is then that it really begins to have implications in our life. We now have enough conviction and desire to be able to base our lives on the Buddha, Dharma, and Sangha in such a way that we actually begin to transform

ourselves in the light of those ideals. It is this level of dedication that is witnessed in someone who becomes a
member of the Western Buddhist Order: commitment to
living out the principles of the Dharma and moving towards spiritual awakening. The person being ordained is
recognized as having a deep enough understanding of
the Buddhist path to be able to base their life around the
Buddha, Dharma, and Sangha, putting all else in relation
to that allegiance. All other aspects of their life are lived
in the light of their devotion to the ideals of Buddhism,
and it is these ideals that guide them and on which they
try to base their life decisions.

Such transformation, if we deepen it through continuing to go for refuge, will eventually lead us to a sustained
experience of spiritual vision. When that awakening has
sufficiently transformed us and the way we respond to
the world, we can say that the goal of the spiritual quest
has started to become a reality. When we establish ourselves in a direct intuitive comprehension of the way
things really are, and that wisdom has sufficiently transformed us, we reach a state from which, traditionally,
there is no falling away, within which there is no forget-
ting what we have seen, no slipping back into the sleep
of spiritual ignorance. All schools of Buddhism speak of
such a state. It is a depth of living out the Three Jewels to
which all Buddhists aspire.

But the final goal of all Buddhists lies beyond even this.
The ideal is realized only in becoming Enlightened
oneself, when intuitive insight into the nature of existence illumines all one's experience and one has entirely

transformed oneself in the light of spiritual awareness. In becoming Enlightened the quest is accomplished. One has become the very embodiment of the Three Jewels.

Ordination marks a commitment to this ever-deepening process. As such, the significance of ordination is not that it marks the end of a journey and a phase of purification, but that it marks the beginning of another journey and a fuller purification.

7

SPIRITUAL DEATH AND REBIRTH

Lo que parte me deja en la ribera
mirando, al mar, la estrella presentida;
lo que llega me anuncia despedida,
ante un vaivén que eterno persevera.

(What departs leaves me on the shore gazing seawards at
the star foreseen; what arrives announces its farewell
before a coming-and-going that goes on for ever.) [38]

The individual who continues the journey from the point of commitment is in many ways a new being. A rite of passage ritualizes this transformation. At the same time it draws out the unending process of death and re-birth inherent to life and consciousness. A spiritual rite of passage inevitably emphasizes the ongoing process within the spiritual quest of letting go of the old and embracing that which is to be – of dying to what one is, in order to be reborn anew.

A NEW NAME

Soon after its birth a baby is given a name. In many other rites of passage the same recognition is accorded to the new person emerging from the transition. Again, when the child becomes an adult a new or additional name is sometimes given, and on getting married a woman sometimes take the name of her husband and they might both receive a new title. People are sometimes given a new name after performing a particularly courageous act. In some traditions the soul of the deceased is given a new name or title to indicate the type of other-worldly spirit they are thought to have become.

Who we are, and what we have been, is largely embodied in our name. Our name is given to us by our parents, and with that name we live and act. Our history imbues that name with a sense of who we are, with a way of being that we (and others) think of as 'us'. The act of ordination, and of going for refuge to the Three Jewels, marks a watershed, with the leaving behind of the old and the establishment of a new approach to life. It is only fitting, therefore, that we also leave behind our old name and take up a new one, a name that embodies our aspirations and the continuing cycle of spiritual death and rebirth upon which we have entered. During the private ordination, therefore, the preceptor gives the ordinand a new name, one that reflects their purpose and the potential that they have undertaken to realize. It is for this reason that I, for example, stopped being Michael and became Moksananda, 'joy of freedom'. I remember my enormous delight at receiving this name, not because I ever disliked my birth name, nor because the name immediately pleased me (in fact, I misheard Sangharakshita and for the first twelve hours or so thought he had called me something else), but because I had been given a name that connected me to the tradition of which I had become a part, and reflected the mysterious quest upon which I had embarked.

In the Western Buddhist Order, the name bestowed at the time of the private ordination is not revealed until the public ordination ceremony, which usually follows some days or weeks later. During this period the ordinand is nameless, nameless to the world, nameless to others. The ordinand has died to who they were and is yet to be reborn. For a time the ordinand sheds all labels, all that is superfluous, and all that designates them as this or that. They are known only to themselves and to their preceptor, with a name that speaks of what is most important. It is a name given to a man, to a woman, but not to a child. It is a name that speaks of life and death and of staring into the universe. It is a name that is not really a name but a path. It is a name with meaning, a name that constantly reminds the ordinand, and others, of the aspiration which it embodies.

The period between the private and public ordinations represents a period during which the new identity of the ordinand is still coming into being. It symbolizes an aspect of the spiritual quest: the ability to gradually free oneself from all definitions and labels, and therefore limitations, and to move constantly towards something new

– even eventually to move on to a state of consciousness beyond all definition whatsoever.

It is said that Siddhārtha, upon attaining Enlightenment, sat under the bodhi tree for seven days before he considered telling others what he had discovered. During that time he assimilated the transformation he had undergone. At first, he seems to have doubted his ability to communicate his experience – whether others would be able to understand. It was only because he was moved by compassion that he decided to try. Having fully assimilated his experience and consequent transformation, he set off in search of his old ascetic friends in order to share with them the path he had discovered. On the way he met Upaka, a seeker after truth.[39] The Buddha was fresh from the seclusion of the place of Enlightenment. He was setting out to roll the wheel of the Dharma, calm, majestic, strikingly present, his eyes bright with newly-seen wisdom. The two wanderers stopped and greeted each other. Upaka was stunned by the presence of the man before him. 'Your form shines like the moon in the night sky. You have the power of understanding. Your eyes are those of a mighty bull. It seems you have achieved your task. Tell me who your teacher is, under whose guidance are you? Whose truth do you profess, who has taught you such happiness?'

But the Buddha, awake to the truth of all things and unshakeable, replied, 'I have no teacher, I venerate no one. I have attained the deathless and am not the same as others. I am an All-transcender, an All-knower, and my like exists nowhere in the world. I have conquered all the forces of ignorance and become free. Now I am on my way to beat the drum of the deathless Dharma, so that others may also be free.'

Unmoved by the lure of fame, free of pride, he looked into the face of Upaka. And Upaka tried to hold him, tried to meet this man who had broken from the confines of the known. He tried to make that leap of imagination. But he couldn't.

'Yes, well. May it be so friend, may it be so.' He looked at the Buddha once more, and then moved on, shaking his head. 'Most remarkable, indeed!' he whispered to himself, looking back over his shoulder in wonderment as he disappeared down the track.

On another occasion a brahmin called Doṇa met the Buddha and was so struck by his appearance that he thought he must be a god.[40] The Buddha denied this.

'A spirit? Some kind of other-worldly being then?' The Buddha denied this also. 'Well, I guess you must be human after all, only …' Doṇa looked back at the Buddha and realized that, no, he wasn't a normal human; he wasn't like any other man.

'I have broken free of all those conditions that would define me as god, spirit, man, or other-worldly being. I am as a lotus broken free of the water. I am not of this world and the world cannot confine me. Take it that I am a Buddha.'

In our own experience there is always something of this inability to really define another person, however much we try. This is particularly true with respect to someone who has recently undergone a spiritual rite of passage, and who continues to fully live out their quest for spiritual vision and transformation. They emerge from the rite of passage as a new being and never quite settle down again. Both they and we need time for this new way of being to be assimilated.

Those returning to the world, after the transition in the wilderness, often experience a period in which they need to absorb that transition, and in which the world too must come to appreciate the being who has returned. Something of the confusion of the period of purification can re-emerge, during which both the ordinand and their friends and family may struggle to make sense of the transition that has taken place, to understand who the new person is and the true significance of the name they have been given, to see more fully the implications of the commitment they have made.

SĀDHANA

Within the ordination ceremony of the Western Buddhist Order spiritual rebirth is not only symbolized with a new name. It also manifests through a particular connection with an archetypal or historical figure who embodies the Enlightened state for which one is striving.

A Buddha lives in complete harmony with reality. Though the word 'Buddha' is used with reference to a historical person who realized this freedom from all existential conflict, it is also used in reference to archetypal Buddhas. These are figures who have emerged within the Buddhist tradition over the centuries. They come from the depths of meditative experience, arising spontaneously from the inspired minds and hearts of those who practise the Buddhist path. A simple way to begin to understand such archetypal images is to think of them as we might imagine someone who has embraced the true nature of existence. Throughout the ages Buddhists have sought to touch Buddhahood using their imagination. They have imagined what it must be like to be a Buddha, and dwelt upon images that conjure up the quality of this way of being. It is a bit like conjuring up the archetype of the wise old man, with his long beard and bright, knowing eyes, or Merlin the magician, or the archetypal King Arthur. By imagining them in the form that best conveys to us their wisdom and understanding, their secret arts, their strength and command, we ourselves get a much better feel for those same qualities.

A Buddha is much more than a wise old man, more even than a magician or king, but by imagining an archetype of a Buddha we begin to get a feel for what it would be like to be a Buddha ourselves. We imagine, for example, a man or woman in the prime of life, sitting crossed-legged in the midst of a vast blue sky, absorbed in meditation, whose appearance and stature convey confidence and intuitive wisdom regarding the nature of existence, and compassion for all beings. We imagine them dressed in rich, colourful silks, perhaps ornamented with jewels, and emanating rainbow light. There are many such archetypal Buddhas and Bodhisattvas and they are reflected upon in some schools of Buddhism in order that one may develop the qualities of a Buddha oneself. They imaginatively represent the goal of our spiritual quest, and the ultimate spiritual rebirth towards which we are moving.

During the private ordination a formal connection is usually made with an Enlightened figure, be it a Buddha, a Bodhisattva, or a great Buddhist teacher of the past. Again, this connection is witnessed by the private preceptor, who will normally formalize this connection by leading the ordinand in the recitation of a mantra. A mantra is a set of sacred syllables associated with the chosen image. The preceptor is able to witness the making of this same connection due to their own connection with the ideal of Buddhahood. Due to their own commitment to become, ultimately, a Buddha, the preceptor can help the ordinand make that same commitment.

The maintenance and development of this connection with Buddhahood, through specific practices, is what we call *sādhana*. This term is in fact quite a complex one in both the Hindu and the Buddhist tradition. Within the Western Buddhist Order the practice of sādhana is generally held to consist of a specific meditation practice through which one makes an effort to move towards Enlightenment. This might involve regular visualization of a historical or archetypal figure, while chanting their mantra and reflecting on their significance and qualities, or it might consist in practising other meditations that help develop the qualities of Buddhahood more generally without reference to any particular figure. In its broadest sense, sādhana might also involve the study of particular texts, associated again perhaps with an archetypal or historical figure, or the conscious development and unfoldment in one's everyday life of spiritual qualities such as mindfulness and compassion. Indeed, all aspects of one's life will ideally form part of the practice of sādhana, as the connection with the goal of Buddhahood is gradually strengthened.

The new name and the sādhana are an immediate embodiment of the commitment that the ordinand makes to an ongoing process of spiritual death and rebirth, and they are important as means through which it is lived out. Through them the constant going forth and going for refuge of the spiritual quest are kept alive: the continual leaving behind of relatively limited ways of being so as to embrace an ever-increasing freedom from all attachment, and an ever-increasing depth of wisdom, breadth of compassion, and continuity of harmony with the universe and with those with whom we share our lives.

8

RETURNING TO THE WORLD

I'd like to get away from earth awhile
And then come back to it and begin over.
May no fate wilfully misunderstand me
And half grant what I wish and snatch me away
Not to return. Earth's the right place for love:
I don't know where it's likely to go better.[41]

Having been separated from the social group in order to
undergo the transition to a new phase of life, social
status, or way of being; having passed through a phase
of purification and preparation; having made a commitment to the new; and having died so as to be reborn, the
individual who undergoes a rite of passage returns to the
world they left behind, just like those who complete the
quest. Perceval eventually became a Grail King, guardian of the Holy Grail, protecting it and the quest for the
well-being of the land and its people. Siddhārtha

returned to the world in order to teach the path to Enlightenment.

No rite of passage is complete until the new individual returns to society. The baby is welcomed from the womb into the community, in some traditions welcomed back as the reincarnation of a former member of the community; the youth takes their place as an adult member of the group; the newly married couple receive the toasts and applause of friends and family and take their place among them; the souls of the dead are often thought to be reunited in a celestial or underworld realm. The rite of passage serves the wider community as well as the individual, and it is celebrated as such. The individual has undergone a rite of passage that expresses, on some level, a mythic transformation. This transformation forms part of a myth that is lived out by the wider community and takes place within that wider context. The return of the individual to the world has meaning for the community too.

The youth of the vision quest lives out the individual myth of finding their guardian spirit. Such a quest, however, forms part of the community's overarching vision of the significance of life and the function of the community. In order to re-enter the community, the transition the individual has undergone must be recognized as such, and must, to some extent, form part of a communal understanding. To begin with, the transformation made by Siddhārtha was so extreme, of such a different order, that it was beyond recognition to those he met. On returning to his ascetic friends, with whom he had previously shared the quest, he was at first unable to convince them of the change he had undergone, even though they were impressed by his appearance and his presence. It was only with time that they were able to understand something of the experience he had had and were able to see him as a Buddha, a fully Enlightened One.

The individual who returns to the world after ordination has not undergone such a radical transformation as the Buddha, but it can still take time for family and friends, as well as the new Order member, to understand the implications of their commitment and the way of life that they have undertaken. Their renewed participation within the wider social group may be recognized by friends, family, and others as being that of a committed Buddhist who forms a part of the Western Buddhist Order. However, it is not always as straightforward as that. For many people the idea of being a Buddhist, particularly an ordained Buddhist with a strange name, is alien and incomprehensible. In any case, many simply don't agree with Buddhist teachings. My father found it very difficult to accept my being a Buddhist and always considered my dedication to Buddhism to be something of a waste of my life. I suspect many of my family, though supportive and showing great kindness and interest, can't help thinking I'm a little bit weird. The Buddhist vision of the meaning of life is not shared by all, and the myth of the spiritual quest that finds expression in the Buddhist tradition is not a myth that informs society as a whole.

The Order member's return to the world is, however, made easier because they join a spiritual community of people who share the same vision. They endeavour to return to the world not as members of their former social group, but as members of the spiritual community of the Western Buddhist Order. Of course, this does not mean they stop being mothers, husbands, daughters, brothers, friends, bosses, or workmates. Nor does it mean they stop being carpenters, schoolteachers, yoga teachers, or accountants. It simply means that they endeavour to interact with others on the basis of their allegiance to the Three Jewels, an allegiance that takes a specific form in their ordination. As Sangharakshita writes,

> Spiritual insight does not consist in seeing new sights with the old eyes but in seeing the old sights with new eyes, just as 'religious' life is not so much a different kind of life as the same old life lived in a new way.[42]

By having friends, fellow members of the Order, who share their vision, aspiration, and commitment, those who make up the Order are more easily able to keep alive the the quest they have undertaken.

This returning to the world, and recognition as a member of the Western Buddhist Order, takes place with the public ordination ceremony. Within a gathering of members of the Order, and sometimes friends and family from outside the Order, the ordinand makes the same commitment they made during the private ordination. This time it is publicly substantiated by the preceptor and witnessed by all those present. In this way they all play their part in the public recognition of the ordinand's transition and, to some extent, the wider significance of what he or she has done.

With the public ordination ceremony the ordinand is welcomed into the Order, most immediately by the public preceptor and some Order members, and through them by all members of the Order. The trust members of the Western Buddhist Order place in the public preceptors means that their substantiation of somebody's commitment to the Three Jewels is accepted by all its members. The individual returns to the world to form a part of a spiritual community, and their transition is understood within a vision of the meaning of life shared by all members of that community. They return to the world not just for their own benefit but for the benefit of others with whom they form the spiritual community, and for the benefit of family, friends, and companions. They return from the 'wilderness' with a greater sense of purpose and meaning, and the positive effect of the rite of passage they have undergone is usually experienced by all. That return is made with an awareness that as individuals they exist not as separate from others but intimately connected to them, and that their own lives form a part of others' lives.

The link between all human beings is given particular emphasis in the Buddhist spiritual community. Through being a part of such a community, intent on developing true sangha, the individuals who constitute it try to give expression to the truth of our interconnectedness with all beings. This idea of interconnectedness is central to

the Western Buddhist Order. However, though it is epit-
omized in the creation of sangha, this is not the only way
in which it is expressed. Ideally, our dealings with others
are based on a deep empathy and a desire to draw out
what is most true, beautiful, and good in each of us and
in mankind as a whole. Many Order members try to
have as positive an influence on the world as possible,
both by working to create spiritual community and by
living out their dedication to the Three Jewels in their in-
teraction with their family and friends. Many also choose
to do so in the midst of their everyday jobs and profes-
sions. For several years, while I was establishing a
Buddhist centre in Valencia, I also worked as an English
teacher, and I very quickly realized that every class I took
was an opportunity to help enrich the lives of my students (just as they enriched my own life). It was well
known among staff and students at the language school
that I was a Buddhist (not least because I used my
Buddhist name) and I think that, although it provoked
curiosity and at times a little cynicism, it engendered
respect and a certain amount of positive self-question-
ing. I remember realizing that quite a few people felt a
sort of pride when I was interviewed about Buddhism
for the newspapers or on television, and a positive connection with the ideals I was communicating.

The idea that we are all interconnected is expressed
within the Western Buddhist Order through the image
of Avalokiteśvara, an archetypal Bodhisattva who works
tirelessly for the awakening of all beings and who embodies the quality of compassion and unconditional

love. Avalokiteśvara is represented as having a thousand arms that work harmoniously to help all beings, and eleven heads to look out to beings in all directions. Similarly, members of the Western Buddhist Order try to work together harmoniously for the sake of others, feeling that our lives and work are interconnected in the same way as the arms of Avalokiteśvara, and together we try to regard all beings just as the eleven heads of the Bodhisattva look out in all directions of space. And, as we have seen, just as Avalokiteśvara is of one heart, a heart of love and compassion, the Order too tries to be of that one heart.

9

THE POWER OF RITES

So, the world happens twice –
once what we see it as;
second it legends itself
deep, the way it is.[43]

With their return to the world the individual's transition is complete; they have died to what they were and been born into the world once again. As we have seen, that return to the world itself marks the beginning of a new phase. A rite of passage is both an end and a beginning.

The baby starts life; the youth begins adulthood; traditionally, the married couple instigates a family; the deceased embarks on an unknown journey. With ordination, the ordinand is ritually established on the Buddhist path and attempts to live out the vision embodied by Avalokiteśvara.

Rites of passage have the power to activate. It is in this sense that they are initiations. At their most effective they set all of oneself in motion so that all one's energies are aligned to the new phase. Rites of passage touch upon the many different aspects of our being and direct them to the new phase. A rite of passage engages our emotions in the transition we undergo, and engages our reason, our will, and our imagination. It involves physical participation and includes the power of speech through our communication. It affects our relationships with others. No part of ourselves is left unaffected by a successful rite of passage.

WORKING IT OUT

Rites of passage therefore have implications for one's life and for the life of the wider community. The implications of ordination in the Western Buddhist Order are most easily understood by looking at the implications of commitment to the Three Jewels.

A member of the Western Buddhist Order is known as a dhammacāri (m.) or dhammacārinī (f.), which means 'one who walks in the Dharma'. Order members attempt to walk the path taught by the Buddha and to course in the infinite openness of the mystery of existence. The rite of passage they have undergone is a symbolic playing out of the quest for spiritual awakening; it is to some extent a rehearsal for Enlightenment. Its many aspects must be worked out upon their return to the world and made a reality. The main question facing any dhammacāri or dhammacārinī is how. Ordination is a purely spiritual act, just as the Order itself is a purely spiritual body. Ordination confers no livelihood as such, nor does it imply a particular lifestyle. There is no easy answer as to how to work out one's quest and one's allegiance to the Buddhist tradition.

Part of the art of an effective spiritual quest is the ability to create contexts that support the living out of one's aspiration in the world. Such an art necessitates flexibility and the ability to respond in an ongoing way to the shifting conditions of life. There is really no prescribed model to follow, no rules to hold on to, only the spirit of going for refuge and the principles of the Dharma.

Yet commitment to the Buddha, the Dharma, and the Sangha does require concrete expression. If we are true to our commitment it will have consequences for how we live and how we interact with other people and the world around us. The individual who returns to society after ordination has changed. Exactly how they manifest that change will become apparent over the succeeding years, and will vary from person to person and from one context to another. Some Order members choose to live a life dedicated primarily to meditation, study, or teaching. Some choose to work within team-based businesses run on Buddhist principles. Others choose to express their commitment through their work within society at large. Some live with fellow members of the Order, some on their own, and some with family or friends. Some live in the quiet of the countryside and some in the midst of the city. There are some who live what amounts to a monastic life, and many Order members live a kind of semi-monastic lifestyle even within the city, establishing single-sex communities with an emphasis on simple conditions for more intensive practice of the Dharma. There are members of the Order who are celibate, others who are not. All of them try to live in conditions that help them live out their aspirations and their commitment to spiritual awakening.

As we saw earlier, rather than follow rules this entails following universal principles. The working out of the commitment made at ordination is guided by a set of ten such principles known as precepts. Whatever their chosen lifestyle, Order members share these precepts as a common expression of their dedication to the Three Jewels and a common foundation for working out that dedication in their lives. The ten precepts are principles in which members of the Order train to live out their ideals ever more deeply. Although rules, policies, systems, regulations, and conventions may be derived from the principles and applied in specific circumstances, the precepts themselves are not formulated as rules. Therefore, each of the precepts can be embodied more or less fully. The skill lies in learning how to apply them from moment to moment and under all conditions.

The principles through which the individual gives effect to their commitment are expressed both in terms of going forth, or leaving behind, and in terms of purification, or the development of ever more emotionally positive and insightful responses to life. A member of the Western Buddhist Order undertakes to go forth from whatever hinders their spiritual growth and to develop what promotes it; to refrain from whatever holds them and others back and to put into practice whatever supports spiritual awakening. It is this double process that is expressed by the ten precepts:

To refrain from harming living beings and to act with loving kindness,

To refrain from taking the not-given and to act with open-handed generosity,

To refrain from any sexual activity that causes harm to others and to practise stillness, simplicity, and contentment,

To refrain from communication that is false and to communicate truthfully,

To refrain from speech that is harsh and to use words that are kindly and gracious,

To refrain from speech that is meaningless and superficial and to communicate in a way that is helpful,

To refrain from backbiting and slander and to promote harmony,

To refrain from covetousness and to develop tranquillity,

To refrain from hatred and to develop compassion,

To refrain from false views and misunderstanding and to develop wisdom.

A lot could be said about these precepts: how they map out the Buddhist path, and the real meaning and implications of each, but to do so would be to embark on an extensive course in Buddhism.[44] It will suffice to say that the full living out of these precepts represents the total transformation of the individual in the light of the ideal of spiritual awakening or Enlightenment. It is these ten precepts that give expression to commitment to the Three Jewels and through which one develops a life dedicated to awakening. Like the arts, the practice of the precepts requires the development of sensitivity, skill, and dedication; it means developing a natural understanding of what assists spiritual development and what does not; it entails learning the subtleties of the application of these principles in everyday life; and it calls for a continued effort to put them into practice. Above all, it requires us to be awake to our experience and present in each and every moment, to remain conscious of our purpose and ever heedful of the many traps of forgetfulness and ineffectiveness into which we might fall. As with any transition undertaken through a rite of passage, the commitment central to that transition must be guarded and nurtured if it is to unfold.

BEYOND ORDINATION

My own admission into the Western Buddhist Order took place many years ago. I remember sitting through the public ordination ceremony feeling focused and energized, experiencing the joy of the event and great happiness at the step I was taking. The ritual itself seemed strangely timeless. None of us being ordained all those years ago knew where it would lead us, but each of us probably felt the joy and freedom of stepping into that unknown. Looking around the room, and hearing the voices of my fellow seekers, I sensed a mood, even a spirit, of companionship. We had gathered in the hall where for the three months of the retreat we had meditated before the shrine, with its polished bronze statue of the Buddha. Our teacher, wearing the rich yellow robes that symbolized his own commitment to the Three Jewels, sat before us, while the former monastery shimmered beneath the vibrant blue of the warm Tuscan sky.

The public ordination ceremony was, obviously, an occasion of great significance for us all. Seriousness was laced with laughter and smiles were set off by the bright eyes of intention. One by one we came forward, bowed before the shrine, and made the triple offering of incense, flower, and candle. Together we requested ordination and together we were ritually purified. Together we made the same commitment that we had made in private, focusing on the essential shared aspiration upon which we had all decided to act. Reciting the three refuges together, we openly dedicated ourselves to the Buddha, the Dharma, and the Sangha, received the kesa, and were welcomed into the Western Buddhist Order.

Sitting in the stillness of the shrine-room after the ceremony, I felt I had set the direction for my life. Though I had been practising Buddhism for some time, and though I had been going for refuge to the Three Jewels for some time, I knew that something more had happened. The simple act of expressing that commitment before my preceptor and the gathered members of the Order, in a ritual that had its roots deep in the tradition I had now joined, had etched that allegiance deep into me and made it more complete. My act of going for refuge to the Buddha, the Dharma, and the Sangha had been witnessed, and I felt it had been witnessed not only by my preceptor and my fellow Order members, but by the Buddha and by all members of his sangha – past, present, and even future.

The years since then have seen my attempt to work out this fundamental Buddhist act of going for refuge. Often foolish, often clumsy, and often lazy in my endeavours, I have continued the process of purification and lived my ongoing death and rebirth. And though my own path has necessarily taken a different route from that of my fellow Order members, and that of Siddhārtha whose example I follow, I sense that through the rite of passage that was my ordination I partake of a myth common to us all.

That myth is the myth of the quest for spiritual awakening. The commitment I made to that universal quest has stayed with me largely through the power of the spiritual rite of passage I underwent in the erstwhile monastery set amid the Tuscan hills. Though many years have passed since I entered the room where I made my own commitment, I have never really forgotten what I touched upon. That small candle-lit room was for a while a sacred spot where I entered upon the universal significance of life, and joined – along with all other Buddhists – Siddhārtha on his quest for the deathless. Those who undergo such an essentially ageless rite find that, in a sense, they never leave the sacred space they enter, just as I have never really left that room. By living out, in this very world, our individual commitment to the quest for awakening – the quest for wisdom and understanding, love and compassion, and a sense of harmony with the way things most truly are – we find that the whole world becomes that sacred space, a place in which we might experience at any moment the ever-present mystery of our own and others' existence.

10

CONCLUSION

E MA O
Dharma wondrous strange.
Profoundest mystery of the Perfect Ones.
In the unmoving, all things come and go,
Yet in that movement nothing ever moves.[45]

Though I have lived for more than forty years, and been a dhammacāri for nearly twenty, I am still unable to say why I should sense that life holds a deep significance. Perhaps it is because that deeper meaning goes beyond all reason. Few would deny in the quiet of their own hearts that we all have moments of wonder when our being vibrates with its echo. As I suggested earlier, we have probably all sensed that life is more, that it is sublime, that it is magical, that it is something far from ordinary, a mystery that – for a few fleeting years – surrounds us, that *is* us.

I have tried to write about beginnings, about the signif icance of the ordination ceremony of the Western Buddhist Order, and about the Buddha, the source of this tradition that we call Buddhism. And I have tried to remind us of life's inherent mystery. In fact, I have referred rather a lot to this mystery. I think this beautifully vague term conveys very well the sense that life ultimately eludes our understanding. It is, quite simply, a mystery.

Mystery is an experience, not an idea, and the sense of mystery we sometimes experience as we contemplate our existence is our own brief, faint glimpse of the deathless. The sense of mystery that sometimes passes over us, or through us, may in fact be the soft brush of the wings of our own spiritual awakening, the momentary falling upon us of the shadow of our true being. And it is often an experience of beauty, the ineffable and transitory beauty of existence itself. Mystery has a sense of beauty to it.

In writing about beginnings, I have written about Siddhārtha and Perceval. These stories touch me not because they are stories of chivalry, gallantry, or heroism, but because they are stories of an individual acting from their aspiration. Many have felt this pressing need to act on those moments in which they sense a call to adventure, a call to understanding and to love, a call to mystery. Of course, not everyone acts on such moments, and perhaps for those who don't there is a life of wondering, of asking 'what if…?', of knowing that the act was lost, that the moment wasn't followed through. But some do; some respond to their heart and go out in search of spiritual adventure, in search of awakening. Of these, some find their path and some don't. Some hold to their aspiration but wander pathless, waiting for that spark to fall from heaven. And who's to say what becomes of them? Some at least whisper to us down the centuries. Only a few find a path and follow it. Some of those are inheritors of a tradition known to modern man as Buddhism. It is a poor word to hold such a message – just another 'ism' after all – but it's all we have.

Inspired by the Buddha's teaching and the example of those who follow it, and with our own aspiration burning within us, those of us who make up this tradition start out on the path of the Dharma. We begin to wander in the forest of the spiritual quest. We meet others capable of teaching us – Buddhists who have been treading the path for some time – and a context that provides the knowledge, experience, and conditions in which to train ourselves. If we are even more fortunate, we may develop the receptivity we need in order to learn.

Of course few Buddhists are as virtuous as those whose example we seek to emulate. Our meanderings often lack direction and decision. Nor yet are we as spiritually mature, and we sometimes turn the ideals to which we aspire into heavy tomes of our own oppression, exchange the wings with which we might fly for iron balls with which to shackle ourselves, walk the path to awakening as if it were yet another road to nowhere. Nonetheless, with perseverance we can make headway and together create a context for that dimension of consciousness and friendship we call sangha.

Men and women of all ages have found it difficult to identify themselves primarily as human beings. It seems much easier to identify ourselves as some category of human being and to identify others likewise, whether in terms of race or nationality, sex, taste, religion, or sect. For that reason I have insisted on the fact that the aspiration that leads individuals to the Western Buddhist Order is not itself Buddhist; it is a human aspiration. The Order attempts to reach beyond conditioning to create a context in which people can relate on the basis of this common aspiration towards understanding the mystery of existence and their common decision to follow the Buddha.

The essence of what it means to be a member of the Order, and therefore what it means to tread the Buddhist path, is embodied in the ceremony that marks entry into it. For those people who constitute the Western Buddhist Order, that ceremony is their common beginning. What it means for each of them unfolds from this ceremony, from the rite of passage it embodies, and from the decisive act of commitment to the Buddha, Dharma, and Sangha that lies at its heart. It is a profoundly significant ceremony, a beginning that holds within its symbolism, and its ritualized form, the quest for and realization of Enlightenment itself.

I think now of my own teacher, Sangharakshita, who ordained me. Like me, he is a man, yet he has tried to stand apart from himself and seems to me to be what he most truly is. That's why I try to listen to him, because he largely stands out of the way of himself and becomes more. I can follow a man like that. 'More and more of less and less,' he has taught, and in doing so he touches on the simple beauty of the Buddhist path. Progress towards the realization of our spiritual aspirations does not consist in learning more and more, or doing more practices, or progressing to higher initiations and secret transmissions, but in understanding at ever deeper levels the essence of the way. It means going ever more deeply into that essence. Any higher teachings are higher only if they actually take us more fully back to the beginning. The real path consists in continually going back to the beginning in order to see more clearly the essence of what we are doing.

The great paradox of the spiritual life is, I suspect, that it is only on completing the journey, the quest, that one realizes that, in a sense, it was unnecessary. We might say that the important thing about the beginning is that it forever holds the end. The beginning is as sublime and as mysterious as that which we seek. The beginning is important because it's through living it ever more fully that we reach the end. The ordination ceremony of the Western Buddhist Order, marking as it does a profound rite of passage, a playing out of the path towards awakening, and someone's entry into the fellowship of the Buddhist tradition, is, for those who pass through it, just such a beginning.

NOTES AND REFERENCES

1 Octavio Paz, 'Más allá del amor', from *The Penguin Book of Spanish Verse*, Penguin Books, Harmondsworth 1956, pp.426–7.

2 Ryokan, *One Robe, One Bowl*, trans. John Stevens, Weatherhill Inc., New York and Tokyo 1984, p.65.

3 In India the Western Buddhist Order is called the Trailokya Bauddha Mahasangha.

4 William Blake, 'The Garden of Love', from *Songs of Experience*.

5 'What is faith (*śraddhā*)? Its nature is that of the purification of mind, which is a profound acquiescence toward and joyful desire for realities, virtues, and abilities.' Hsüan-tsang, *Demonstration of Consciousness Only*, trans. Francis H. Cook, Numata Center for Buddhist Translation and Research, Berkeley, CA 1999, p.173.

6 Basho, *Basho Haiku*, trans. Lucien Stryk, Penguin Books, 1995, p.1.

7 This threefold going for refuge is traditionally repeated in Pali:

Buddhaṃ saraṇaṃ gacchāmi.
Dhammaṃ saraṇaṃ gacchāmi.
Saṅghaṃ saraṇaṃ gacchāmi.

8 See, for example, the *Vāseṭṭha Sutta*:

Then Vāseṭṭha and Bhāradvāja said to the Buddha: 'It is amazing, Venerable Gotama, it is wonderful, Venerable Gotama! Just as if one might raise what has been overturned, or reveal what has been hidden, or point out the way to him who has gone astray, or hold out a lamp in the dark so that those who have eyes may see objects, so likewise has the Truth been explained by Venerable Gotama in various ways. Therefore, we take refuge in him, his Dhamma and his Sangha. May the Venerable Gotama accept us as lay followers who henceforth have taken refuge in him for the rest of our lives.' H. Saddhatissa (trans.), *Vāseṭṭha Sutta*, verse 63, from the *Sutta-Nipāta*, Curzon Press, London 1985, p.75.

9 An early example of instructions for such a ceremony can be found at *Vinaya Piṭaka* i.12:

Let the one to be ordained get the hair of the head and face shaved off. Let him get the saffron robes put upon him. Let him put the upper robe over one shoulder, salute the feet of the brethren, sit down in a squatting posture, stretch out folded palms, and let him thus say:
'To the Buddha I go for refuge.
To the Norm I go for refuge.
To the Order I go for refuge.'
(Thrice.)

> I enjoin, brethren, that ordination and full orders do consist in going to these Three Refuges.
>
> (*Vinaya* i.12, in *Some Sayings of the Buddha*, trans. F.L. Woodward, Buddhist Society, London 1974, p.36.)

10 Sangharakshita, *The Ten Pillars of Buddhism*, Windhorse Publications, Birmingham 1996, p.43. Sangharakshita founded the Western Buddhist Order in the UK in 1968. For a full account of how and why he started the Order see his books, *The History of My Going for Refuge* and *Moving Against the Stream*; also Subhuti, *Bringing Buddhism to the West* and *Sangharakshita: A New Voice in the Buddhist Tradition*.

11 Arnold van Gennep, *The Rites of Passage*, Routledge and Kegan Paul, London 1960.

12 D.H. Lawrence, from 'Song of a Man who has Come Through', *Selected Poems*, Penguin, Harmondsworth 1972, p.84.

13 For a thorough account of the Arthurian legends visit the 'Mystical World Wide Web' (http://www.mystical-www.co.uk/arthuriana2z).

14 Sangharakshita (trans.), *Dhammapada* 85, Windhorse Publications, Birmingham 2001.

15 Sangharakshita, *A Survey of Buddhism*, Windhorse Publications, Birmingham 2001, p.103.

16 For example, *Ariyapariyesanā Sutta, Majjhima Nikāya* 26.

17 *Lalitavistara* 19.

18 A.D. Hope, from 'Tiger', quoted in *The Rattle Bag*, ed. Seamus Heaney and Ted Hughes, Faber and Faber, London 1982, pp.430–1.

19 C.G. Jung, 'The Symbolic Life', in *Collected Works*, trans. R.F.C. Hull, Princeton University Press, Princeton, 1953–79, volume 18, par. 630.

20 James Hollis, *Under Saturn's Shadow*, Inner City books, Toronto 1994, p.17.

21 'The first stage of passage was *separation*, physical separation from the parents in order to begin the psychological separation. This was never a matter of choice for the boy. Often, in the middle of the night, he would be "kidnapped" from his parents by the gods or the demons, the older men of the tribe who wore masks or painted their faces. These masks moved them from the familiar realm of neighbors or uncles to the status of gods or archetypal forces'. James Hollis, *Under Saturn's Shadow*, op. cit., p.17.

22 Śāntideva, *A Guide to the Bodhisattva's Way of Life*, trans. Stephen Batchelor, Library of Tibetan Works and Archives, Dharamsala 1979, chapter 9 verses 56–9, pp.143–4.

23 H. Saddhatissa (trans.), *Pabbajjā Sutta*, from the *Sutta-Nipāta*, op. cit., p.47.

24 *Vatthūpama Sutta, Majjhima Nikāya* 7.

25 See Kulananda, *Teachers of Enlightenment*, Windhorse Publications, Birmingham 2000.

26 The private and the public preceptor can be the same person, though this is increasingly uncommon.

27 Śāntideva, *A Guide to the Bodhisattva's Way of Life*, op. cit., chapter 3, verses 26–7, p.33.

28 For an illuminating discussion of the distinction between the group and the spiritual community, and the role of the individual in each, see Sangharakshita, *What is the Sangha?* Windhorse Publications, Birmingham 2000.

29 Sangharakshita, 'Getting Beyond the Ego' in *Crossing the Stream*, Windhorse Publications, Birmingham 1996, p.205.

30 Śāntideva, *A Guide to the Bodhisattva's Way of Life*, op. cit., chapter 1, verse 25, p.14.

31 *Metta Sutta (Sutta-Nipāta* 149), trans. F.L. Woodward, in *Some Sayings of the Buddha*, op. cit., p.44.

32 Sangharakshita, 'The Way of Emptiness', from *Crossing the Stream*, op. cit., p.212.

33 Sangharakshita, *A Survey of Buddhism*, op.cit, p.439.

34 Milarepa, from 'The Bandit-Disciple', *The Hundred Thousand Songs of Milarepa*, trans. Garma C.C. Chang, Shambhala Publications, Boston and London 1999, p.157.

35 This parable is told in the eighth chapter of the *Saddharma Puṇḍarīka Sūtra (Lotus Sūtra)*.

36 Rainer Maria Rilke, from *Letters to a Young Poet*, trans. M.D. Herton Norton, W.W. Norton and Co., New York 1962, p.35.

37 C.G. Jung, 'Symbols of Transformation', in *Collected Works*, op.cit., volume 5, par. 551.

38 Alberto Álvarez Quintero, from 'Ante el Mar', prose trans. J.M. Cohen, *The Penguin Book of Spanish Verse*, op.cit., p.431.

39 *Ariyapariyesanā Sutta, Majjhima Nikāya* 26.

40 *Aṅguttara Nikāya* 4.36.

41 Robert Frost, from 'Birches', *The Rattle Bag*, op. cit., p.79.

42 Sangharakshita, 'The Good Friend', from *Crossing the Stream*, op. cit., p.61.

43 William Stafford, 'Bifocal', from *The Rattle Bag*, op. cit., p.76.

44 See Sangharakshita, *The Ten Pillars of Buddhism*, op. cit.

45 Translated from a Mahāyāna sādhana in Sangharakshita's possession.

FURTHER READING

Joseph Campbell, *The Power of Myth*, Bantam Doubleday Dell, 1988

Mircea Eliade, *The Sacred and Profane: The Nature of Religion*, Harcourt, Australia 1968

Arnold van Gennep, *The Rites of Passage*, University of Chicago Press, 1961

Kulananda, *Teachers of Enlightenment*, Windhorse Publications, Birmingham 2000

Sangharakshita, *Forty-Three years ago: Reflections on my Bhikkhu Ordination*, Windhorse Publications, Birmingham 1993

Sangharakshita, *Moving Against the Stream*, Windhorse Publications, Birmingham 2003

Sangharakshita, *The History of My Going for Refuge*, Windhorse Publications, Birmingham 1988

Sangharakshita, 'The Journey to Il Convento' in *The Priceless Jewel*, Windhorse Publications, Birmingham 1993

Sangharakshita, *The Ten Pillars of Buddhism*, Windhorse Publications, Birmingham 1996

Sangharakshita, *What is the Sangha?* Windhorse Publications, Birmingham 2000

Subhuti, *Bringing Buddhism to the West*, Windhorse Publications, Birmingham 1995

Subhuti, *Sangharakshita: A New Voice in the Buddhist Tradition*, Windhorse Publications, Birmingham 1994

Vessantara, *Meeting the Buddhas*, Windhorse Publications, Birmingham 1993

INDEX

The Windhorse symbolizes the energy of the enlightened mind carrying the Three Jewels – the Buddha, the Dharma, and the Sangha – to all sentient beings.

Buddhism is one of the fastest-growing spiritual traditions in the Western world. Throughout its 2,500-year history, it has always succeeded in adapting its mode of expression to suit whatever culture it has encountered.

Windhorse Publications aims to continue this tradition as Buddhism comes to the West. Today's Westerners are heirs to the entire Buddhist tradition, free to draw instruction and inspiration from all the many schools and branches. Windhorse publishes works by authors who not only understand the Buddhist tradition but are also familiar with Western culture and the Western mind.

Manuscripts welcome.

For orders and catalogues vist www.windhorsepublications.com or contact

WINDHORSE PUBLICATIONS
11 PARK ROAD
BIRMINGHAM
B13 8AB
UK

WINDHORSE BOOKS
PO BOX 574
NEWTOWN
NSW 2042
AUSTRALIA

WEATHERHILL INC
41 MONROE TURNPIKE
TRUMBULL
CT 06611
USA

Windhorse Publications is an arm of the Friends of the Western Buddhist Order, which has more than sixty centres on five continents. Through these centres, members of the Western Buddhist Order offer regular programmes of events for the general public and for more experienced students. These include meditation classes, public talks, study on Buddhist themes and texts, and 'bodywork' classes such as t'ai chi, yoga, and massage. The FWBO also runs several retreat centres and the Karuna Trust, a fund-raising charity that supports social welfare projects in the slums and villages of India.

Many FWBO centres have residential spiritual communities and ethical businesses associated with them. Arts activities are encouraged too, as is the development of strong bonds of friendship between people who share the same ideals. In this way the fwbo is developing a unique approach to Buddhism, not simply as a set of techniques, less still as an exotic cultural interest, but as a creatively directed way of life for people living in the modern world.

If you would like more information about the FWBO visit the website at www.fwbo.org or write to

LONDON BUDDHIST CENTRE	SYDNEY BUDDHIST CENTRE	ARYALOKA
51 ROMAN ROAD	24 ENMORE ROAD	HEARTWOOD CIRCLE
LONDON	SYDNEY	NEWMARKET
E2 0HU	NSW 2042	NH 03857
UK	AUSTRALIA	USA

ALSO FROM WINDHORSE

KULANANDA

PRINCIPLES OF BUDDHISM

Buddhism is one of the most popular religions of today – its teachings on kindness, simplicity, and interconnectedness are attracting many people disenchanted with the world's all-pervading consumerism.

This simple guide holds the essential teachings and methods of practice to help bring these qualities alive. The author, Kulananda, a practising Buddhist for 28 years, shows us how this approach to life can make a real difference to us and our capacity to grow clearer, wiser, and happier.

160 pages
ISBN 1 899579 59 1
£5.99/$8.95/€8.95

BODHIPAKSA

VEGETARIANISM

Part of a series on *Living a Buddhist Life*, this book explores connections between vegetarianism and the spiritual life.

As a trained vet, Bodhipaksa is well placed to reveal the suffering of animals in the farming industry, and as a practising Buddhist he can identify the ethical consequences of inflicting such suffering. Through the Buddhist teaching of interconnectedness he lays bare the effects our eating habits can have upon us, upon animals, and upon the environment.

He concludes that by becoming vegetarian we can affirm life in a very clear and immediate way, and so experience a greater sense of contentment, harmony, and happiness.

112 pages
ISBN 1 899579 15 X
£4.99/$7.95/€7.95

JINANANDA

MEDITATING

This is a guide to Buddhist meditation that is in sympathy with modern lifestyle. Accessible and thought-provoking, this books tells you what you need to know to get started with meditation, and keep going through the ups and downs of everyday life. Realistic, witty, and very inspiring.

128 pages
ISBN 1 899579 07 9
£4.99/$7.95/€7.95

SANGHADEVI

LIVING TOGETHER

Living Together explores the essential ingredients of community living, including friendliness, cooperation, meaningful communication, and mutual vision.

Drawing on her many years in Buddhist communities, Sanghadevi, a widely-respected Buddhist teacher, encourages those who aspire to this lifestyle to engage with the frequent challenges they will encounter and speaks from her experience of the joys of sharing.

112 pages
ISBN 1 899579 50 8
£4.99/$7.95/€7.95

KULANANDA

TEACHERS OF ENLIGHTENMENT

THE REFUGE TREE OF THE WESTERN BUDDHIST ORDER

Out of the depths of a clear blue sky emerges a beautiful tree of white lotus flowers. On the tree are many figures – historical, mythical, and transcendental – each a teacher of Enlightenment. This is the Refuge Tree: a compelling image which, in its many different forms, has inspired Buddhists for centuries.

Here, Kulananda explains the significance of the figures on the Refuge Tree of the Western Buddhist Order. These teachers, each in their own way, have all changed the world for the better, playing a part in the creation of the rich Buddhist tradition we know today.

304 pages, with illustrations and b&w photos
ISBN 1 899579 25 7
£12.99/$21.95/€21.95

ŚĀNTIDEVA

THE BODHICARYĀVATĀRA

A GUIDE TO THE BUDDHIST PATH TO AWAKENING

The *Bodhicaryāvatāra*, one of the best-loved Buddhist texts, tells of a noble ideal: a compassionate life lived for the well-being of the world. Through his uplifting verses Śāntideva, the eighth-century monk and poet, depicts the training of the Bodhisattva and evokes the sublime desire to bring an end to all suffering.

This new translation by Kate Crosby and Andrew Skilton comes with an introduction by the translators, explanatory notes, and an introduction by Paul Williams.

320 pages
ISBN 1 899579 49 4
£12.99/$16.95/€16.95

PADMASURI

TRANSFORMING WORK

AN EXPERIMENT IN RIGHT LIVELIHOOD

Transforming Work shows how our work can be meaningful and creative, and an integral part of any vibrant spiritual practice.

This book profiles Windhorse:evolution, a multi-million pound Buddhist giftware business which gives away most of its profits. The personal stories found here explore the vision of Right Livelihood, part of the Buddha's Noble Eightfold Path, in practice.

'Although primarily addressed to Buddhists, *Transforming Work* could well provide a wake-up call for all those seeking to find value in their lives. With generosity of spirit, Padmasuri presents a clear introduction to the subject and, inadvertently, how it feels to live a Buddhist life in today's world.'
John Lane, author of *Timeless Simplicity*

256 pages with photographs
ISBN 1 899579 52 4
£9.99/$14.95/€14.95